The
EVERYTHING®
Word Games Challenge Book

Dear Reader:

Your fun is my main goal for this book. But it is more than just that. Years ago I wrote a collection of computer games that were based on traditional ideas. Computerized versions of games like Jacks and Pickup Sticks were both familiar and entertaining. But I thought that they could be improved in two ways: first by allowing people to compete against one another rather than just playing solo, and second, by offering some redeeming value beyond training players to point and click really fast. Based on what I learned, I decided that word puzzles would be the ideal type of game.

So I created ✐ *www.funster.com*, a Web site dedicated to word games. It offers everything: a place to play familiar word games with others or alone, some educational value, and most importantly, fun (as the name "Funster" would suggest). This book attempts to offer you all of this based on many of the tried-and-true games that continue to make Funster a popular destination for wordplay.

If you have half as much fun solving these puzzles as I have had creating them, then my goal will be accomplished. Enjoy!

Charles Timmerman

The EVERYTHING® Series

Editorial

Publishing Director	Gary M. Krebs
Managing Editor	Kate McBride
Copy Chief	Laura M. Daly
Acquisitions Editor	Kate Burgo
Development Editor	Christina MacDonald
Production Editors	Jamie Wielgus
	Bridget Brace

Production

Production Director	Susan Beale
Production Manager	Michelle Roy Kelly
Series Designers	Daria Perreault
	Colleen Cunningham
	John Paulhus
Cover Design	Paul Beatrice
	Matt LeBlanc
Layout and Graphics	Colleen Cunningham
	John Paulhus
	Daria Perreault
	Monica Rhines
	Erin Ring
Series Cover Artist	Barry Littmann

Visit the entire Everything® Series at *www.everything.com*

THE

EVERYTHING®

Word Games Challenge BOOK

750 scramblers, anagrams, acrostics, and more

Charles Timmerman

Adams Media
Avon, Massachusetts

For Suzanne and Calla.

An Everything® Series Book.
Everything® and everything.com® are registered trademarks of F+W Publications, Inc.

Published by Adams Media, an F+W Publications Company
57 Littlefield Street, Avon, MA 02322 U.S.A.
www.adamsmedia.com

ISBN 10: 1-59337-312-0
ISBN 13: 978-1-59337-312-2
Printed in the United States of America.

J I H G F E D C

Library of Congress Cataloging-in-Publication Data
Timmerman, Charles.
The everything word games challenge book / Charles Timmerman.
p.   cm.
(An everything series book)
ISBN 1-59337-312-0
1. Word games. I. Title. II. Series: Everything series.

GV1507.W8T47 2005
793.73'4—dc22
                          2004030877

This publication is designed to provide accurate and authoritative information with regard to the subject matter covered. It is sold with the understanding that the publisher is not engaged in rendering legal, accounting, or other professional advice. If legal advice or other expert assistance is required, the services of a competent professional person should be sought.

—From a *Declaration of Principles* jointly adopted by a Committee of the American Bar Association and a Committee of Publishers and Associations

Many of the designations used by manufacturers and sellers to distinguish their products are claimed as trademarks. Where those designations appear in this book and Adams Media was aware of a trademark claim, the designations have been printed with initial capital letters.

This book is available at quantity discounts for bulk purchases.
For information, please call 1-800-289-0963.

Contents

Acknowledgments

I would like to thank each of the half a million or so people who have visited my Web site, *www.funster.com*, to play word games. You are the ones who put the fun into Funster, and now into this book.

A special thanks to my agent Jacky Sach for providing this opportunity to discover that writing a word game book really is as much fun as it sounds.

I am grateful for the assistance from the fine folks at Adams Media. It was a pleasure working with my editors Kate Burgo and Christina MacDonald.

Funster and *What's in a Name?* are trademarks of Charles Timmerman.

Top Ten Word Challenges
in This Book

1. Discover ancient riddles and their answers buried in history.

2. Phone Numbers show you how to code and decode secret messages using your telephone.

3. Cryptarithms get your brain into shape with word arithmetic.

4. Chronograms reveal how dates are hidden in ancient inscriptions on buildings and tombstones.

5. Play Word Know-It-All and impress your friends with an expanded vocabulary.

6. Try your hand at Word Ladders, a popular word game invented by the author Lewis Carroll.

7. Acrostics are the precursor to the modern crossword puzzle.

8. Try What's in a Name? the most popular game at *www.funster.com*.

9. Liven up any party by playing Inky Pinkys.

10. Magically transform words into other words with Logogriphs.

Introduction

▶ With all of the entertainment options available today, why do people still play word games? It turns out that there are some very good reasons why wordplay remains popular. It isn't just that people are trying to be retro cool, although many of the games in this book might have been played by your grandparents' grandparents (and they just might have been better at them than you are).

One thing word games have going for them is that they require your *active* participation, which is a refreshing change from the growing trend toward passive entertainment. There once was a time when people actually played sports rather than watched them, made up stories rather than turned on the television, and even sang songs rather than put on a CD. You can enjoy most books by passively reading the pages, but here you will be required to actively participate by working the puzzles!

Word games can also bring people together socially, something that is less common as we spend more time at home watching television. Most of the games in this book can be played with others—family at home, friends at parties, strangers on a bus, the kids in the car—whoever, wherever. Word games are portable and no expensive equipment is required. People of all ages and from all walks of life can play together.

Mental exercise is another thing that word games offer. Let's face it; a neural workout is not the goal of most modern forms of entertainment. But research shows that mental exercise is important to keep your brain fit, just as physical exercise keeps your body in shape.

Contrary to popular belief, recent studies indicate that with mental exercise your brain can continue to grow as you age. Word games are a fun way to get your daily mental workout.

And you just might learn something practical by playing word games. Of course, words are the fundamental building blocks of human communication. So the more you know about words and how to use them, the more effective you can be at communicating with others. Many of the puzzles in this book will help build your vocabulary and expand your word power.

People enjoy word games because they are a form of play. As every child instinctively knows, play is important business and a way to experiment and explore our world in a safe environment. Even babies enjoy wordplay, delighting with the repetition and rhymes of words and sounds. Word games give us a way to play again, something that is often left behind as we grow older.

For all of these reasons people have been enjoying wordplay for thousands of years, in all cultures of the world. You will learn some of the history of the word games presented in this book. The games are all the more fun knowing that people generations ago enjoyed the same word challenges.

One thing you should know about the puzzles in this book is that they were not designed for word geniuses. You might be able to solve some of the puzzles in a matter of seconds, while others might take hours of thought and repeated attempts. This book presents a smorgasbord of word challenges, so there should be something for nearly everyone.

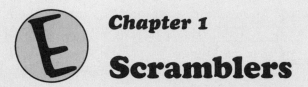

Chapter 1

Scramblers

Do you like order in your life? Well then, you'll love these puzzles. Each one comes complete with all of the letters and words found in the solution. The trick is that they have been scrambled in some way. Find out how good you are at turning chaos into order.

Unscramble the Words in These Quotes

Unscramble the letters to form words, then put the words in the appropriate blanks to complete a quote. (Answers for this section begin on page 284.)

Example:

"The _____ of _____ is to do _____

_____ _____ well."

—*John D. Rockefeller*

- NCOOMM
- EESCRT
- MNOYLMCONU
- SESSUCC
- HITSNG

The answer is:

"The secret of success is to do common things uncommonly well."

—*John D. Rockefeller*

Knocking at Your Door

"A _____ sees the _____ in every _____;

an _____ sees the _____ in every _____."

—*Sir Winston Churchill*

- IFYILUDFTC
- RTUYPNPTOOI
- ESIPISTMS
- OINUYPPOTRT
- CUITFLDIYF
- IIMPTOST

Hard Work

" _____ is one _____ _____ and

ninety-nine _____ _____."

—*Thomas Edison*

- ENSUIG
- TASPNIIIONR
- PNTREEC
- INSRIPPOARTE
- CERTPNE

The Good Life

" _____ like no one is _____. _____

like no one is _____. _____ like you've never been

_____ and _____ like it's _____

on _____."

—*Mark Twain*

- CDNAE
- ANEHEV
- LOEV
- LEIV
- ANWGHICT

- NGIS
- HUTR
- ARTEH
- ETINLSING

Fairness

"_____ _____ is a _____ to

_____ _____ ."

—*Martin Luther King, Jr.*

- TNCSEIIUJ
- IUECSTJ
- YAENEWHR
- RTAETH
- HYVEEEWERR

Elementary

"When you have _____ the _____ , that which

_____ , _____ _____ , must be

the _____ ."

—*Sir Arthur Conan Doyle*

- PSLBOSMIEI
- UTHTR
- PBIREBMAOL
- RHVEEWO
- AEILIETMDN
- MAISENR

Wise Words

"Better to _____ _____ and be _____

a _____, than to _____ and _____

all _____."

—*Abraham Lincoln*

- LINTSE
- REEMOV
- FLOO
- INAMER
- OTGHUHT
- PKASE
- DUOTB

Indebted

"We do not _____ the _____ from our _____,

we _____ it from our _____."

—*Ancient Indian Proverb*

- RCEDHNLI
- RIITNHE
- AHETR
- SSORTEACN
- OBRORW

Motivation

"The _____ for a _____ _____

_____ is to have _____ it."

—*Ralph Waldo Emerson*

- READRW
- ODEN
- NHTIG
- LLEW
- EDNO

My Friend

"I _____ _____ a _____ that was so

_____ as _____."

—*Henry David Thoreau*

- PONIMOCAN
- SLTEDUIO
- ERENV
- ENOANPCLABOMI
- DFUON

Come to Me

" _____ is as a _____ which, when _____,

is always _____ our _____, but which if you will

_____ down _____, may _____ upon you."

—*Nathaniel Hawthorne*

- TALIHG
- PURSUDE
- YELTTFBRU
- SAGRP
- SPINHEPSA
- TSI
- YIQTULE
- BDNOYE

 ## Unscramble the Words in These Categories

Unscramble the letters to form words. All of the words in each group belong in the given category. (Answers for this section begin on page 284.)

Example:

Chess Pieces

1. EUEQN
2. OHSPIB
3. HNTGKI

The answers are:

1. QUEEN
2. BISHOP
3. KNIGHT

Countries

1. UCIAGAARN   _____

2. ENETLETNICISH   _____

3. MEKADRN   _____

4. NACDAA   _____

5. FITGNNASAHA   _____

Birds

1. GNMIRBCIKOD   _____

2. RRPASOW   _____

3. RIOLOE   _____

4. EPAEKATR   _____

5. LDCAANRI   _____

Kitchen Items

1. OCRAPBUD   _____

2. DBERNLE   _____

3. FREGITERRORA   _____

Kitchen Items—continued

4. EVTSO   _____

5. EVNO   _____

Vegetables

1. ERAIHCOKT   _____

2. OCLOBRCI   _____

3. PGSAAASUR   _____

4. IDRSAH   _____

5. AIPCSHN   _____

Airplane

1. NIGEEN   _____

2. IWGN   _____

3. CITPOCK   _____

4. TALI   _____

5. TIOLP   _____

Insects

1. UYTRTFBLE   _____

2. RAYFGNOLD   _____

3. LGYABUD   _____

4. RPRSOAPSGEH   _____

5. QUOMISOT   _____

Sports

1. GIOXBN   _____

2. RTEISGWNL   _____

3. CKCIERT   _____

4. BWIOGLN   _____

5. LLVLAYELOB   _____

Gems

1. RELMEAD   _____

2. PLOA   _____

3. NTRGAE   _____

Gems—continued

4. IPEHRPSA _____

5. EIOQUTUSR _____

Condiments

1. TLSA _____

2. STCUPA _____

3. NRRGAIMEA _____

4. TASRMUD _____

5. HDERSHROSAI _____

Dances

1. ISTTW _____

2. WZALT _____

3. LHSTUE _____

4. MLOBI _____

5. NEMGREEU _____

Reassemble the Letter Blocks

Rearrange these blocks of letters to form phrases. (Answers for this section begin on page 285.)

Example:

S-A

ICT

RDS.

-PA

INT

AND

URE

-WO

-TH

OUS

A-P

The answer is:

A-PICTURE-PAINTS-A-THOUSAND-WORDS.

To Your Health	How Much?	Precious
LE-	-FR	IND
CTO	FE-	THI
AY-	THI	LE-
A-D	EE.	TE.
PS-	-IN	RIB
WAY.	-LI	TO-
THE	THE	A-M
KEE	-BE	TER
AN-	ST-	-IS
-DO	NGS	-A-
R-A	ARE	WAS
APP		NG-

Missing You	*Picky*	*Look Inside*
E-M	LED	-JU
ENC	MAN	K-B
HEA	T-F	COV
ER.	-BU	-CA
AKE	ARE	-A-
RT-	CAL	TS-
HE-	RE-	YOU
OND	-CH	Y-I
S-T	N.	DGE
GRO	OSE	BOO
W-F	EW-	ER.
ABS	Y-A	N'T

Heartbreaker		*Meow*	*Golden*
-AT	-TO	Y-T	ULD
N-N	R-T	HE-	-WO
VE-	AVE	ILL	-HA
L.	THA	N-T	-YO
ST-	-AL	WHE	NTO
-LO		CAT	YOU
AND		AY.	UNT
LOV		MIC	THE
-LO		'S-	O-U
VED		HE-	THE
ED-		-PL	O-O
O-H		E-W	RS-
EVE		AWA	U.
-HA			DO-
BET			AS-
TER			VE-
			M-D

Rearrange the Words in These Quotes

Unscramble the order of these words to form quotes. You will need to add the appropriate capital letters and punctuation. (Answers for this section begin on page 285.)

Example:
"forgive err to to is divine human"

—Alexander Pope

The answer is:
"To err is human, to forgive divine."

—Alexander Pope

Imagine That

"you it if it can you dream can do"

—Walt Disney

Age

"a regrets place the is until take old not of man dreams"

—John Barrymore

Good Morning

"man healthy wise to a to early and rise bed and wealthy makes early"

—*Benjamin Franklin*

Empty

"know I is one and I know only thing that nothing that"

—*Socrates*

Be Nice

"kindness act small wasted ever of how no matter is no"

—*Aesop*

Order

"minds consistency foolish little a of the hobgoblin is"

—*Emerson*

Happiness

"when assume object is that can life the happy men be do of they happiness only not"
—*George Orwell*

Highways and Byways

"in roads two the took I diverged that all one less the has a I made traveled and and wood by difference"

—*Robert Frost*

Deception

"time the of the people the the the the can time people cannot fool you people and time all some but fool of all some you all all"

—*Abraham Lincoln*

Glow

"smile of your of smile the sometimes source joy the your joy be sometimes but source your is your can"

—*Thich Nhat Hanh*

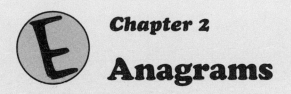

Chapter 2

Anagrams

Rearrange all of the letters in one word or phrase to form another word or phrase, and you have an anagram. People have been playing around with anagrams for thousands of years. In the third century B.C. the Greek poet Lycophron scored points by transposing the king's name into a phrase that meant "made of honey." See if you are as clever with these anagram challenges.

Anagrams of Famous People

Rearrange the letters in these words to form famous names. (Answers for this section begin on page 285.)

Example:

Presidents

The answers are:

1. HUG GORES WEB

2. MARRY JIM ETC

3. VETOED HORSE LOOTER

1. George W. Bush

2. Jimmy Carter

3. Theodore Roosevelt

Country Singers

1. OH JAN SYNCH _____

2. HAD LARGER GEM _____

3. ONLY TOLD RAP _____

4. SHORT GRAB OK _____

5. TINY PLACES _____

Baseball Players

1. TUBA HERB _____

2. EIGHT PALACES _____

3. JOCKS AGREEING _____

4. I AGE GOOD JIM _____

5. A MILKY CEMENT _____

Jazz Musicians

1. SIT ON A CUBE _____

2. BE BRAVE DUCK _____

3. A SNOWMAN LYRIST _____

4. CHALK REPAIRER _____

5. MORTALS SOURING _____

Football Coaches

1. DARN MY LOT _____

2. CIVIL DOBERMAN _____

3. OPERA ON JET _____

Football Coaches—continued

4. HOLD A SUN   _____

5. NO KEEN TRUCK   _____

Fashion World

1. ORANGE ORIGAMI   _____

2. NICKEL ANVIL   _____

3. TONAL YARN   _____

4. FLIGHTY MEMOIR   _____

5. UNREAL COIL BIZ   _____

Astronauts

1. EARLY LIDS   _____

2. ALTERING NORMS   _____

3. GISMOS RUGS   _____

4. ASHLAND PEAR   _____

5. UNBLIZZARD   _____

Boxers

1. MAIL A MUD HAM _____

2. MY JADE SPECK _____

3. NO MEAGER GOFER _____

4. MONEY SKIT _____

5. MAKE A JOLT AT _____

Scientists

1. TINIEST ENABLER _____

2. A KNIGHTS NEPHEW _____

3. DANISH CRAWLER _____

4. VALID INROAD ONCE _____

5. TAIWAN SCONE _____

Quarterbacks

1. CAR STORAGE HUB _____

2. EGO BRIBES _____

3. ATE NOON JAM _____

Quarterbacks—continued

4. NEAR FRONT TANK _____

5. ONE HAT JAM _____

Western Movie Stars

1. OLD WEST ACTION _____

2. SORRY GORE _____

3. WHEN NO JAY _____

4. NO SOCK CRUNCH _____

5. NEATER GUY _____

Comedians

1. CARTS BY LILLY _____

2. ANY JOEL _____

3. LEND JERSEY FIR _____

4. LIAR WINS LIMBO _____

5. A VERMIN TEST _____

Anagrams of Places

Rearrange the letters in these words to form names of places. (Answers for this section begin on page 286.)

Example:

Florida Cities

1. JAVELIN LOCKS

2. FEATURED DOLLAR

3. A LETHAL SEAS

The answers are:

1. Jacksonville

2. Fort Lauderdale

3. Tallahassee

Mountains

1. HUMANS TOAST

_____

2. SKIP A KEEP

_____

3. OVERSEEN MUTT

_____

4. HARM ROTTEN

_____

5. DRAGON TENT

_____

Hoosier Cities

1. EVIL NAVELS

_____

2. AIDS PAIN LION

_____

Hoosier Cities—continued

3. LONG MOON BIT   _____

4. LAY AT FEET   _____

5. OFTEN AWRY   _____

Asian Countries

1. I MET VAN   _____

2. HAD LATIN   _____

3. OAK SHOUTER   _____

4. ALIAS AMY   _____

5. PLANE   _____

Lakes

1. A TEAK HOLE   _____

2. LOUISE PARKER   _____

3. LATERAL GASKET   _____

4. ELK AERIE   _____

5. ORIENTAL OAK   _____

California Cities

1. OCEAN SMART

   _____

2. LEGAL NOSES

   _____

3. CASINO FRANCS

   _____

4. AS JONES

   _____

5. DIAGNOSE

   _____

Islands

1. ENGLANDER

   _____

2. A-OK LIMO

   _____

3. TRAUMAS

   _____

4. GAGS A OPAL

   _____

5. HARVESTMAN DIARY

   _____

Canadian Cities

1. TOO TORN

   _____

2. TERM LOAN

   _____

3. NOVA CURVE

   _____

Canadian Cities—continued

4. RACY GAL _____

5. PINE WING _____

European Countries

1. MEG RYAN _____

2. I NAPS _____

3. I AS A RUT _____

4. DINERS WALTZ _____

5. DO PLAN _____

Space

1. ARMS _____

2. SUN RAT _____

3. RUN USA _____

4. TEEN PUN _____

5. HEART _____

New England

1. MUST STASH ACES _____

2. CUT CENT COIN _____

3. I NAME _____

4. ASHEN WHIMPER _____

5. HAND SOLDIER _____

Universities

1. RUDE UP _____

2. MORE DANTE _____

3. NO EGG TOWER _____

4. DARN SOFT _____

5. TEEN PANTS _____

Texas Cities

1. ALL SAD _____

2. SHOUT ON _____

3. IS A NUT _____

Texas Cities—continued

4. ANOINT A SON _____

5. SO PALE _____

 # *Anagram Pairs*

Determine the missing word in each sentence by rearranging the letters in another word found in the same sentence. (Answers for this section begin on page 286.)

Example:

1. To truly listen, you must be _____.

2. Praise those who _____ for a better world.

The answers are:

1. To truly **listen**, you must be SILENT.

2. **Praise** those who ASPIRE for a better world.

Politics

1. The senator was found guilty of _____ .

2. The _____ strove to impeach him.

3. We should devote all of our efforts to getting this bill _____.

4. Sometimes the _____ politicians can end up being the most hostile.

Rent

1. She was one of the tannest _____ in the apartment.

2. "Each unit comes with _____," rasped the landlord.

3. Don't worsen the situation by telling the _____.

4. The house was _____ with legal tender.

5. One more caveat: You must _____ on thirty days' notice.

Toddlers

1. Do not despair, your little one will not wear _____ forever!

2. The toddler used _____ paper to make a toy animal.

3. The little slugger _____ every time he hits the ball.

Insects

1. The _____ stung the king while he sat on his throne.

2. The unnamed insect was a rather _____ example of a centipede.

3. The slug sensed _____ in the garden.

4. The boater used _____ to remove the roaches from his yacht.

Art

1. The _____ was largely responsible for the artist's success.

2. The sculptor's popularity soared when the critic said that she _____ him.

3. Daniel _____ the blue ribbon right onto the artwork.

Food

1. The _____ in the food agrees with him.

2. A pointer for your diet: Eat more _____ .

3. He was hired as a _____ of the bakery's treats.

Work

1. The labor is _____ but he enjoys being outside.

2. The workers are tearing _____ out of the hill.

3. Andrew works as a _____ .

4. The fireman _____ back at the station when the bell clanged.

5. The _____ who lost the accounts shall remain nameless.

High Seas

1. Even the _____ water has a subtle hue of green.

2. The airman was out of place in the _____.

3. He was hoarse from shouting at all of the people who went _____.

4. He paddled across the ocean in a _____.

5. The _____ was kept free of trash.

School Rules

1. A _____ will be disciplined by the teacher.

2. Never assume that your chatting _____ the teacher.

3. _____ do not fall asleep during my lecture.

4. The grader of the exam will have little _____ for incomplete answers.

Construction

1. The property has been zoned for a _____ buildings.

2. As a general rule, you will not be able to _____ your house.

3. The hardest part was when they _____ the building site.

4. He was always dreaming of a mansion but built a _____ house.

Writing

1. He braved his teacher's wrath and used an _____ instead of an adjective.

2. There is nothing dopier than using a _____ in the middle of a sentence.

3. She was editing a manuscript about _____.

4. The caveman wrote about the battle on his _____.

Family Ties

1. She _____ her secret admirer.

2. The settler wrote _____ back to his family.

3. Remember when our _____ used to smother us with kisses?

Farm

1. Gosh, there are a lot of _____ on a farm!

2. Many of the framers of the constitution were also _____.

3. The thirsty _____ wandered down to the shore.

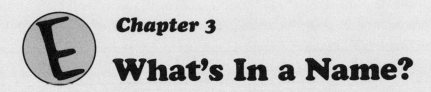

Chapter 3

What's In a Name?

What's In a Name? is a popular word game for people of all ages. Many people find it addictive because the concept is simple and familiar: find words using only the letters in a given name. What's In a Name? is similar to anagrams, except not all of the letters in a name need to be used each time. As you will discover, to make the game more challenging, just start looking for longer words.

Find the Four-Letter Words

Find four-letter words (the clean ones!) using only the letters in a given name. Each letter in a name can be used only once within your word. In the back of this book there are many possible words for each name. (Words that are always capitalized or require a hyphen or an apostrophe are not included in the lists. Words with variant or British spellings are also not included.) Your challenge is to find 10 four-letter words per name. (Answers for this section begin on page 288.)

Example:
Tom Brokaw

Possible answers are:
amok, atom, bark, boar, boat, book, boom, boor, boot, brat, brow, kart, mark, mart, moat, moor, moot, okra, roam, rook, room, root, taro, tomb, took, tram, warm, wart, womb, work, worm

Gary Player

1. _____

2. _____

3. _____

4. _____

5. _____

6. _____

7. _____

8. _____

9. _____

10. _____

Quincy Jones

1. _____

2. _____

3. _____

4. _____

5. _____

6. _____

7. _____

8. _____

9. _____

10. _____

Burl Ives

1. _____

2. _____

3. _____

4. _____

5. _____

6. _____

7. _____

8. _____

9. _____

10. _____

James Dean

1. _____

2. _____

3. _____

4. _____

5. _____

6. _____

7. _____

8. _____

9. _____

10. _____

Lena Horne

1. _____

2. _____

3. _____

4. _____

5. _____

6. _____

7. _____

8. _____

9. _____

10. _____

Helen Hayes

1. _____
2. _____
3. _____
4. _____
5. _____

6. _____
7. _____
8. _____
9. _____
10. _____

W. C. Fields

1. _____
2. _____
3. _____
4. _____
5. _____

6. _____
7. _____
8. _____
9. _____
10. _____

Greta Garbo

1. _____

2. _____

3. _____

4. _____

5. _____

6. _____

7. _____

8. _____

9. _____

10. _____

Jerry Lewis

1. _____

2. _____

3. _____

4. _____

5. _____

6. _____

7. _____

8. _____

9. _____

10. _____

Bear Bryant

1. _____

2. _____

3. _____

4. _____

5. _____

6. _____

7. _____

8. _____

9. _____

10. _____

 ## *Find the Five-Letter Words*

Find five-letter words using only the letters in a given name. See the beginning of this chapter for the rules. Your challenge is to find 7 five-letter words per name. (Answers for this section begin on page 288.)

Example:
Woodrow Wilson

Possible answers are:
dolor, donor, doors, downs, drool, drown, idols, irons, lions, loins, loons, lords, odors, rinds, roils, rondo, roods, rosin, snood, solid, swirl, swoon, sword, sworn, widow, wilds, winds, winos, woods, wools, words, world

Clark Gable

1. _____

2. _____

3. _____

4. _____

5. _____

6. _____

7. _____

8. _____

9. _____

10. _____

Evelyn Waugh

1. _____

2. _____

3. _____

4. _____

5. _____

6. _____

7. _____

8. _____

9. _____

10. _____

Lauren Bacall

1. _____

2. _____

3. _____

4. _____

5. _____

6. _____

7. _____

8. _____

9. _____

10. _____

Lionel Richie

1. _____

2. _____

3. _____

4. _____

5. _____

6. _____

7. _____

8. _____

9. _____

10. _____

Richard Pryor

1. _____

2. _____

3. _____

4. _____

5. _____

6. _____

7. _____

8. _____

9. _____

10. _____

Jimmy Connors

1. _____

2. _____

3. _____

4. _____

5. _____

6. _____

7. _____

8. _____

9. _____

10. _____

John Gielgud

1. _____

2. _____

3. _____

4. _____

5. _____

6. _____

7. _____

8. _____

9. _____

10. _____

Alice Walker

1. _____

2. _____

3. _____

4. _____

5. _____

6. _____

7. _____

8. _____

9. _____

10. _____

Bob Marley

1. _____

2. _____

3. _____

4. _____

5. _____

6. _____

7. _____

8. _____

9. _____

10. _____

Willie Nelson

1. _____

2. _____

3. _____

4. _____

5. _____

6. _____

7. _____

8. _____

9. _____

10. _____

Find the Six-Letter Words

Find six-letter words using only the letters in a given name. See the beginning of this chapter for the rules. Your challenge is to find 5 six-letter words per name. (Answers for this section begin on page 289.)

Example:
Daniel Boone

Possible answers are:
albino, bailed, baleen, banned, beadle, beaned, beanie, belied, binned, blonde, boiled, bonnie, debone, denial, doable, edible, enable, inland, leaden, leaned, linden, loaned, nailed, noodle

Tanya Tucker

1. _____

2. _____

3. _____

4. _____

5. _____

Gore Vidal

1. _____

2. _____

3. _____

4. _____

5. _____

Fran Tarkenton

1. _____

2. _____

3. _____

4. _____

5. _____

Lionel Richie

1. _____

2. _____

3. _____

4. _____

5. _____

George Burns

1. _____

2. _____

3. _____

4. _____

5. _____

Boris Becker

1. _____

2. _____

3. _____

4. _____

5. _____

Gale Sayers

1. _____

2. _____

3. _____

4. _____

5. _____

Bill Moyers

1. _____

2. _____

3. _____

4. _____

5. _____

Gerald R. Ford

1. _____

2. _____

3. _____

4. _____

5. _____

Ray Charles

1. _____

2. _____

3. _____

4. _____

5. _____

Find the Seven-Letter Words

Find seven-letter words using only the letters in a given name. See the beginning of this chapter for the rules. Your challenge is to find 4 seven-letter words per name. (Answers for this section begin on page 289.)

Example:
Isaac Newton

Possible answers are:
actions, ancient, anoints, canines, cantina, consent, contain, inanest, incants, intones, nascent, nations, notices, octanes, satanic, section, tension, townies, wannest, wantons

John Coltrane

1. _____

2. _____

3. _____

4. _____

James Earl Jones

1. _____

2. _____

3. _____

4. _____

Ted Williams

1. _____

2. _____

3. _____

4. _____

Bryant Gumbel

1. _____

2. _____

3. _____

4. _____

Charlie Parker

1. _____

2. _____

3. _____

4. _____

Carole King

1. _____

2. _____

3. _____

4. _____

Andrew Greeley

1. _____

2. _____

3. _____

4. _____

Rod Serling

1. _____

2. _____

3. _____

4. _____

Loretta Young

1. _____

2. _____

3. _____

4. _____

Arthur Godfrey

1. _____

2. _____

3. _____

4. _____

Find the Eight-Letter Words

Find eight-letter words using only the letters in a given name. See the beginning of this chapter for the rules. Your challenge is to find 3 eight-letter words per name. (Answers for this section begin on page 290.)

Example:
Katharine Hepburn

Possible answers are:

aberrant, abrupter, aperture, bankrupt, banterer, breather, brethren, earthier, hankerer, harkener, heartier, herniate, inerrant, inherent, inurbane, parakeet, partaken, partaker, pretrain, preunite, prurient, renature, retainer, reuniter, terrapin, tinkerer, turnpike, unbeaten, urbanite

Raymond Chandler

1. _____

2. _____

3. _____

Eric Dickerson

1. _____

2. _____

3. _____

Gabriel García Márquez

1. _____

2. _____

3. _____

Thelonious Monk

1. _____

2. _____

3. _____

Alistair Cooke

1. _____

2. _____

3. _____

Oscar Robertson

1. _____

2. _____

3. _____

Greg Louganis

1. _____

2. _____

3. _____

Alec Guinness

1. _____

2. _____

3. _____

Abner Doubleday

1. _____

2. _____

3. _____

Steve Martin

1. _____

2. _____

3. _____

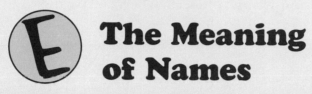

Chapter 4

The Meaning of Names

Maybe a rose by another name would smell as sweet. And perhaps sticks and stones might break my bones while names will never hurt me. But then again, names are a powerful part of our lexicon. The word games in this chapter explore the origins and meanings of different names.

Name that Famous Person

Have you ever wanted to change your name? Marion Michael Morrison changed his name to John Wayne and became one of the toughest cowboys in Hollywood. In each of the following groups, match each famous name in the left column with the corresponding birth name in the right column. (Answers for this section begin on page 291.)

Male Singers

John Denver •   • Richard Starkey

Ringo Starr •   • Henry John Deutschendorf, Jr.

Ice-T •   • Gordon Sumner

Elton John •   • Reginald Kenneth Dwight

Sting •   • Tracy Marrow

Female Singers

Joni Mitchell •   • Eleanora Fagan

Tina Turner •   • Roberta Joan Anderson

Patsy Cline •   • Mary Isobel Catherine O'Brien

Billy Holiday •   • Virginia Patterson Hensley

Dusty Springfield •   • Anna Mae Bullock

Actors

Alan Alda • • Ramon Estevez

Martin Sheen • • Frank James

George Burns • • Alphonso D'Abruzzo

Gary Cooper • • Thomas Mapother IV

Tom Cruise • • Nathan Birnbaum

Actresses

Judy Garland • • Gladys Smith

Mary Pickford • • Norma Jean Baker

Marilyn Monroe • • Edna Gilhooley

Ellen Burstyn • • Margarita Cansino

Rita Hayworth • • Frances Gumm

Sports

Ahmad Rashad • • Ferdinand Lewis Alcindor, Jr.

Rocky Marciano • • Johnny Lee

Kareem Abdul-Jabbar • • Rocco Francis Marchegiano

Hulk Hogan • • Terry Gene Bollea

Johnny Bench • • Bobby Moore

Pen Names

Lewis Carroll •   • John Wilson

George Orwell •   • Charles Lutwidge Dodgson

Mark Twain •   • Eric Arthur Blair

Dr. Seuss •   • Theodore Geisel

Anthony Burgess •   • Samuel Langhorne Clemens

 # Name These Animals

There are many ways to name an animal. Each of the following challenges requires you to match an animal in the left column with its corresponding term in the right column. (Answers for this section begin on page 292.)

Groups of Birds

Penguins •   • A convocation

Quail •   • A bevy

Buzzards •   • An exaltation

Eagles •   • A wake

Larks •   • A colony

Groups of Mammals

Lions •	• A clan
Oxen •	• A business
Apes •	• A pride
Ferrets •	• A shrewdness
Hyenas •	• A yoke

Groups of Insects

Flies •	• An intrusion
Locusts •	• A plague
Grasshoppers •	• A colony
Cockroaches •	• A business
Ants •	• A cloud

Animal Adjectives

Ass •	• Taurine
Bee •	• Apian
Bird •	• Asinine
Bull •	• Avian
Cat •	• Feline

Female Names

Deer •   • Jenny

Ferret •   • Hen

Donkey •   • Cow

Elephant •   • Hob

Lobster •   • Doe

Male Names

Pigeon •   • Bull

Bison •   • Cock

Horse •   • Gobbler

Pig •   • Stallion

Turkey •   • Boar

Offspring

Moose •   • Kid

Cougar •   • Calf

Goat •   • Chick

Kangaroo •   • Joey

Ostrich •   • Kitten

Name These Phobias

There are many things to be afraid of and just as many names for these fears. For the following puzzles, match the phobia in the left column with the corresponding object of the fear in the right column. (Answers for this section begin on page 292.)

To Your Health

Dermatophobia •   • Fear of going to the doctor

Cardiophobia •   • Fear of vomiting

Pathophobia •   • Fear of heart disease

Iatrophobia •   • Fear of skin disease

Emetophobia •   • Fear of disease

Insects and Animals

Arachnophobia •   • Fear of reptiles

Ichthyophobia •   • Fear of birds

Ornithophobia •   • Fear of spiders

Herpetophobia •   • Fear of bees

Apiophobia •   • Fear of fish

Don't Go Outside

Aerophobia •   • Fear of the moon

Lunaphobia •   • Fear of snow

Noctiphobia •   • Fear of fresh air

Limnophobia •   • Fear of lakes

Chinophobia •   • Fear of the night

Other People

Androphobia •   • Fear of crowds

Venustraphobia •   • Fear of men

Pedophobia •   • Fear of robbers

Harpaxophobia •   • Fear of beautiful women

Ochlophobia •   • Fear or dislike of children

Objects

Crystallophobia •   • Fear of machinery

Bacillophobia •   • Fear of missiles

Bibliophobia •   • Fear of glass

Cyberphobia •   • Fear of books

Mechanophobia •   • Fear of computers

Names by Category

In each of the following groups, match a name in the left column with its corresponding definition in the right column. (Answers for this section begin on page 293.)

Latin Names for Trees

Populus grandidentata •

Ulmus rubra •

Acer rubrum •

Acer saccharum •

Juniperus virginiana •

• Sugar maple

• Red elm

• Red maple

• Eastern red cedar

• Bigtooth aspen

Medical Names for Body Parts

Popliteal •

Hallux •

Sclera •

Vomer •

Pollex •

• Slender bone between nostrils

• Thumb

• Big toe

• Hollow in back of knee

• White of eye

Occupation Names

Wright •   • Sawer of wood

Webster •   • Bricklayer

Sawyer •   • Operates looms

Mason •   • One who repairs things

Glazier •   • Window glassman

Names for Colors

Azure •   • Orange yellow

Russet •   • Sky blue

Saffron •   • Reddish brown

Glaucous •   • Violet

Mauve •   • Sea green

Names for Measurements

Decibel •   • Unit of force

Parsec •   • Unit used to measure depth of water

Dyne •   • Unit for sound intensity

Fathom •   • Unit of fatality

Megadeath •   • Unit of interstellar distance

Names with Common Endings

In each of the following groups, match a name in the left column with its corresponding definition in the right column. (Answers for this section begin on page 293.)

Doctrines (-ism)

Accidentalism •   • Belief that pleasure is the main goal in life

Hedonism •   • Theory that events do not have causes

Solipsism •   • Belief in the existence of God

Optimism •   • Theory that self-existence is the only certainty

Theism •   • A doctrine that this is the best possible world

Government (-cracy)

Democracy •   • Government by divine guidance

Meritocracy •   • Government by children

Paedocracy •   • Government selected by ability

Aristocracy •   • Government by the people

Theocracy •   • Government by the nobility

Divination (-mancy)

Necromancy •   • Divination by walking in a circle until dizzy

Crystallomancy •   • Divination by gazing into a reflective object

Bibliomancy •   • Divination by conjuring up the dead

Ichthyomancy •   • Divination by opening a book at random

Gyromancy •   • Divination by looking at fish entrails

Obsessions (-mania)

Xenomania •   • Obsession with yourself

Bibliomania •   • Obsession with stealing

Kleptomania •   • Obsession with books

Megalomania •   • Obsession with foreign things

Egomania •   • Obsession with grandiose behavior

Sciences (-ology)

Biology •   • Study of human movement

Hypnology •   • Study of life

Kinesiology •   • Study of the environment

Ecology •   • Study of handwriting

Graphology •   • Study of sleep

Shapes (-form)

Boviform •   • Kidney-shaped

Reniform •   • Ox-shaped

Cuneiform •   • Star-shaped

Stelliform •   • Wedge-shaped

Guttiform •   • Drop-shaped

Knowledge (-osophy)

Misosophy •   • Universal knowledge

Philosophy •   • Knowledge of being

Anthroposophy •   • Hatred of knowledge

Ontosophy •   • Knowledge of human development

Pansophy •   • Science of knowledge

Feeding (-orous)

Insectivorous •   • Feeding on grain

Carnivorous •   • Feeding on insects

Granivorous •   • Feeding on bread

Baccivorous •   • Feeding on animals

Panivorous •   • Feeding on berries

Lovers (-phile)

Bibliophile •   • Lover of high-fidelity sound

Audiophile •   • Lover of God

Sinophile •   • Lover of books

Hippophile •   • Lover of horses

Theophile •   • Lover of China and Chinese culture

Polygons (-gon)

Hexagon •   • Polygon with twelve sides

Isagon •   • Polygon with fifteen sides

Dodecagon •   • Polygon with six sides

Quindecagon •   • Polygon with nine sides

Nonagon •   • Polygon whose angles are equal

Chapter 5

Logogriphs

Medieval alchemists tried to transform base metals into gold—an exciting idea that failed. With logogriphs it actually is possible to transform one word into another. The puzzles in this chapter involve a number of transformation methods. No magic is required, just a sharp knowledge of words.

Beheadments

To "behead" a word, remove the first letter and form a new word. In the following puzzles, solve the clues to determine the word pairs. You will need to behead the first word in order to form the second word. (Answers for this section begin on page 294.)

> *Example:*
> Behead something used to climb and get a viper.
>
> The answer is *ladder* and *adder.*

Behead to Make **H** Words

1. Behead a pair of dark glasses and get the underworld. _____ _____

2. Behead this part of a car and get the bottom of a shoe. _____ _____

3. Behead this seasoning and get an itchy skin problem. _____ _____

4. Behead sharp tips on a stem and get sharp tips on a head _____ _____

Behead to Make **C** Words

1. Behead a fastener and get a group of workmen. _____ _____

2. Behead oak fruit and get something that grows on ears. _____ _____

3. Behead a graphic symbol and get a swindle. _____ _____

4. Behead an odor and get a coin. _____ _____

Behead to Make **P** Words

1. Behead saliva and get a hole in the ground. _____   _____

2. Behead an empty area and get a rate of movement. _____   _____

3. Behead a sharp projection and get a fish. _____   _____

4. Behead a tournament and get a writing instrument. _____   _____

5. Behead a gemstone and get a close friend. _____   _____

Behead to Make **A** Words

1. Behead a shoe cord and get a hotshot. _____   _____

2. Behead a place frequently visited and get your mom's sister. _____   _____

3. Behead a skin growth and get a product of creativity. _____   _____

4. Behead a place to raise pigs and get a limb. _____   _____

5. Behead a forest official and get mad. _____   _____

Behead to Make **U** Words

1. Behead a painful toe condition and get an organization of employees. _____   _____

2. Behead a drug dealer and get a theater escort. _____   _____

3. Behead a liquid mover and get a baseball official. _____   _____

Behead to Make **T** Words

1. Behead a long narrow piece and get a journey.   _____ _____

2. Behead a circular island get a road fee.   _____ _____

3. Behead a length of wood and get a tapping sound.   _____ _____

4. Behead a celestial body and get a heavy dark substance.   _____ _____

5. Behead a tiny particle and get a male cat.   _____ _____

Behead to Make **L** Words

1. Behead an air trip and get an illumination.   _____ _____

2. Behead an eye movement and get a piece of a chain.   _____ _____

3. Behead a hand garment and get a strong positive emotion.   _____ _____

4. Behead fatty tissue and get a scientist's workplace.   _____ _____

5. Behead a small fastener and get backtalk.   _____ _____

Behead to Make **R** Words

1. Behead a car operator and get a stream.   _____ _____

2. Behead a beverage and get a place for skating.   _____ _____

3. Behead a decorative pin and get a pest.   _____ _____

Behead to Make **R** Words—continued

4. Behead a baby's bed and get a bone.   _____ _____

5. Behead a criminal and get a chess piece.   _____ _____

Behead to Make **E** Words

1. Behead a creature to get this direction.   _____ _____

2. Behead a metal joiner to get an older person. _____ _____

3. Behead a feeling of fear to make a mistake.   _____ _____

4. Behead the prince of darkness to get his spirit. _____ _____

Behead to Make **I** Words

1. Behead someone who plunders and get angry.   _____ _____

2. Behead soft thin paper and get a vital matter. _____ _____

3. Behead the sound that a pig makes and get a
    printing liquid.   _____ _____

4. Behead small rodents and get something frozen. _____ _____

5. Behead a songbird and get a unit of measurement. _____ _____

Curtailments

To "curtail" a word, remove the last letter of a word to form another word. In the following puzzles, solve the clues to determine the word pairs. You will need to curtail the first word in order to form the second word. (Answers for this section begin on page 295.)

Example:
Curtail a large gathering and get a bird.

The answer is *crowd* and *crow*.

Curtail These **M** Words

1. Curtail a partner and get a pad. _____ _____

2. Curtail the average and get a means of communication. _____ _____

3. Curtail this satellite and get the sound of a cow. _____ _____

4. Curtail the list of dishes and get adult males. _____ _____

5. Curtail anger and get mom. _____ _____

Curtail These **B** Words

1. Curtail a place for money and get a decree. _____ _____

2. Curtail an alcoholic beverage and get a flying insect. _____ _____

3. Curtail a stomach and get something that rings. _____ _____

4. Curtail a length of wood and get a swine. _____ _____

5. Curtail a recognizable name and get parts of grain. _____ _____

Curtail These **H** *Words*

1. Curtail this feeling of dislike and get something
   for your head.   _____ _____

2. Curtail a group of females and get a rabbit.   _____ _____

3. Curtail a golden-brown color and get a cloudy appearance._____ _____

Curtail These **D** *Words*

1. Curtail a place to unload a boat and get a medical
   practitioner.   _____ _____

2. Curtail a person who acts and get a female deer. _____ _____

3. Curtail a depression and get an animal's home.   _____ _____

4. Curtail something owed and get a female name.   _____ _____

Curtail These **S** *Words*

1. Curtail a form of wrestling and get the result of addition. _____ _____

2. Curtail an old writing tablet and get a thin strip of wood. _____ _____

3. Curtail a slant and get pig food.   _____ _____

4. Curtail a carbonated drink and get a ground covering. _____ _____

5. Curtail a place to sit and get a body of water.   _____ _____

Curtail These **K** Words

1. Curtail a toy that flies and get a model to be assembled.   _____   _____

2. Curtail a ruler and get relatives.   _____   _____

3. Curtail a game of chance and get a male name.   _____   _____

Curtail These **G** Words

1. Curtail a fool and get a messy substance.   _____   _____

2. Curtail monotonous work and get a smile.   _____   _____

3. Curtail a complaint and get a grasp.   _____   _____

4. Curtail a mark of performance and get a person who has received a degree.   _____   _____

5. Curtail a wound and get a fuel.   _____   _____

Curtail These **C** Words

1. Curtail a block and get a baseball player.   _____   _____

2. Curtail an ice cream holder and get a swindle.   _____   _____

3. Curtail a person who is gullible and get a close friend.   _____   _____

4. Curtail a place to hang coats and get a conclusion.   _____   _____

5. Curtail a part of your face and get a letter of the Greek alphabet.   _____   _____

Syncopations

To "syncopate" a word, remove one of the middle letters of a word to form another word. In the following puzzles, solve the clues to determine the word pairs. You will need to syncopate the first word in order to form the second word. (Answers for this section begin on page 295.)

Example:
Syncopate a U.S. territory and get something you chew.

The answer is *Guam* and *gum*.

Syncopate These **L** *Words*

1. Syncopate this espresso drink and get tardy.   _____ _____

2. Syncopate a blastoff and get a midday meal.   _____ _____

3. Syncopate a slot machine arm and get a sheet.   _____ _____

4. Syncopate wingless parasites and get a fib.   _____ _____

5. Syncopate an upper floor and get a portion of land.   _____ _____

Syncopate These **T** *Words*

1. Syncopate a string and get the surface of a tire.   _____ _____

2. Syncopate a path and get the last part.   _____ _____

3. Syncopate a heading and get a flat slab.   _____ _____

4. Syncopate a musical note and get a digit.   _____ _____

Syncopate These **D** Words

1. Syncopate a stadium roof and get a female deer. _____ _____

2. Syncopate a feeling of terror and get someone who is inanimate. _____ _____

3. Syncopate one who gives and get a swinging barrier. _____ _____

Syncopate These **P** Words

1. Syncopate a device to inflate objects and get a young dog. _____ _____

2. Syncopate a dramatic work and get a remuneration. _____ _____

3. Syncopate a pillar and get a plant holder. _____ _____

Syncopate These **S** Words

1. Syncopate shredded cabbage and get a hand tool. _____ _____

2. Syncopate a milky drink and get a Japanese alcoholic beverage. _____ _____

3. Syncopate an animal's hard covering and get a store's activity. _____ _____

4. Syncopate a part of a bookcase and get you. _____ _____

5. Syncopate a poor urban area and get the whole amount. _____ _____

Syncopate These **B** *Words*

1. Syncopate an infant and get a shoreline indentation.   _____   _____

2. Syncopate a lure and get a flying mammal.   _____   _____

3. Syncopate a curved segment and get a piece
    of furniture.   _____   _____

4. Syncopate a color and get the rear side.   _____   _____

Syncopate These **W** *Words*

1. Syncopate part of an airplane and get a head covering.   _____   _____

2. Syncopate labor and get a Chinese pan.   _____   _____

3. Syncopate a twisting and get a literary activity.   _____   _____

Syncopate These **R** *Words*

1. Syncopate an incline and get a form of music.   _____   _____

2. Syncopate a sport and get a gem.   _____   _____

3. Syncopate a part in a play and get fish eggs.   _____   _____

4. Syncopate an elevation and get a lift.   _____   _____

Transadditions

To "transadd" a word, first add a letter to a given word, and then rearrange all of the letters to form another word. In the following puzzles, transadd each word according to the clues. (Answers for this section begin on page 295.)

Example:
Transadd this word: Beer
Add an *M* and make a word for ash.

The answer is *ember.* (rearrange the letters B E E R M)

Transadd This Word: **Retain**

1. Add a *C* to make sure. _____

2. Add an *S* to make a filter. _____

3. Add a *P* to make one who coats your house. _____

4. Add an *L* to make a toilet. _____

5. Add an *H* to make something worn on the head. _____

Transadd This Word: **Horse**

1. Add an *A* to go on land. _____

2. Add a *C* to make some work. _____

3. Add an *N* to get wading birds. _____

4. Add a *D* to get crowds. _____

Transadd This Word: **Teach**

1. Add an *L* to get a Swiss dwelling. _____

2. Add an *S* to get a perfume packet. _____

3. Add a *C* to get a seal of approval. _____

Transadd This Word: **Cereal**

1. Add a *V* to get a butcher's knife. _____

2. Add a *D* to make a statement. _____

3. Add a *P* to substitute. _____

4. Add a *T* for something excessively sweet. _____

5. Add an *N* for someone who will remove dirt. _____

Transadd This Word: **Earth**

1. Add a *B* to get someone who is wet. _____

2. Add a *T* to get one who makes head coverings. _____

3. Add an *F* to get a male parent. _____

4. Add an *L* to get a woman's top. _____

Transadd This Word: **Lace**

1. Add a *B* to get a cord.   _____

2. Add a *T* to get a shoe projection.   _____

3. Add an *M* to get a desert animal.   _____

4. Add a *D* to get a sticker.   _____

Transadd This Word: **Star**

1. Add a *B* to get annoying children.   _____

2. Add an *E* to get the charges.   _____

3. Add an *F* to get flat boats.   _____

4. Add a *C* to get wagons.   _____

Transadd This Word: **Love**

1. Add a *W* to get *A*, E, I, O, U.   _____

2. Add an *N* to get a work of fiction.   _____

3. Add an *S* to find the answer.   _____

4. Add an *I* to get a Mediterranean fruit.   _____

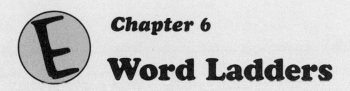

Chapter 6

Word Ladders

Word Ladders were devised by Lewis Carroll, author of *Alice's Adventures in Wonderland*. He introduced them as Doublets in *Vanity Fair* on March 29, 1879. They became so popular that the magazine had a weekly competition. As you will discover, these puzzles can be tackled starting from either end of the ladder.

Three-Letter Word Ladders

Link these three-letter words together with a ladder of words. Each step in the ladder must be a real word, and must differ from the previous word by only one letter. There are many possible solutions, but try to use only the given number of steps. (Answers for this section begin on page 296.)

Example:

CAT to DOG

The answer is:

C	**A**	**T**
C	O	T
D	O	T
D	**O**	**G**

PIG to STY

This word ladder was given to the readers of *Vanity Fair* by Lewis Carroll.

P	I	G
___	___	___
___	___	___
___	___	___
___	___	___
S	T	Y

SAD to JOY

S	A	D
_____	_____	_____
_____	_____	_____
J	O	Y

FOG to SUN

F	O	G
_____	_____	_____
_____	_____	_____
_____	_____	_____
S	U	N

OWL to FOX

O	W	L
_____	_____	_____
_____	_____	_____
_____	_____	_____
F	O	X

JOG to RUN

J   O   G

_____   _____   _____

_____   _____   _____

R   U   N

OLD to NEW

O   L   D

_____   _____   _____

_____   _____   _____

_____   _____   _____

_____   _____   _____

_____   _____   _____

_____   _____   _____

N   E   W

ICE to HOT

I   C   E

_____   _____   _____

_____   _____   _____

_____   _____   _____

_____   _____   _____

_____   _____   _____

H   O   T

ONE to TWO

O   N   E

_____   _____   _____

_____   _____   _____

_____   _____   _____

_____   _____   _____

_____   _____   _____

_____   _____   _____

T   W   O

TOP to END

T   O   P

_____ _____ _____

_____ _____ _____

_____ _____ _____

_____ _____ _____

_____ _____ _____

E   N   D

ARM to LEG

A   R   M

_____ _____ _____

_____ _____ _____

_____ _____ _____

_____ _____ _____

L   E   G

JET to FLY

J   E   T

_____   _____   _____

_____   _____   _____

_____   _____   _____

_____   _____   _____

F   L   Y

DRY to WET

D   R   Y

_____   _____   _____

_____   _____   _____

_____   _____   _____

W   E   T

PAL to FOE

P	A	L
_____	_____	_____
_____	_____	_____
_____	_____	_____
F	O	E

NEW to OLD

N	E	W
_____	_____	_____
_____	_____	_____
_____	_____	_____
_____	_____	_____
_____	_____	_____
_____	_____	_____
O	L	D

Four-Letter Word Ladders

Link these four-letter words together with a ladder of words. Each step in the ladder must be a real word, and must differ from the previous word by only one letter. There are many possible solutions, but try to use only the given number of steps. (Answers for this section begin on page 296.)

Example:

HEAD to TAIL

The answer is:

H	**E**	**A**	**D**
H	E	A	L
T	E	A	L
T	E	L	L
T	A	L	L
T	**A**	**I**	**L**

FOUR to FIVE

This word ladder was given to the readers of *Vanity Fair* by Lewis Carroll.

F	O	U	R
___	___	___	___
___	___	___	___
___	___	___	___
___	___	___	___
___	___	___	___
F	I	V	E

SAND to DUNE

S	A	N	D
_____	_____	_____	_____
_____	_____	_____	_____
_____	_____	_____	_____
D	U	N	E

WILD to TAME

W	I	L	D
_____	_____	_____	_____
_____	_____	_____	_____
_____	_____	_____	_____
_____	_____	_____	_____
T	A	M	E

HATE to LOVE

H	A	T	E
_____	_____	_____	_____
_____	_____	_____	_____
L	O	V	E

WARM to COLD

W	A	R	M
___	___	___	___
___	___	___	___
___	___	___	___
C	O	L	D

SEED to TREE

S	E	E	D
___	___	___	___
___	___	___	___
___	___	___	___
___	___	___	___
T	R	E	E

MORE to LESS

M	O	R	E
___	___	___	___
___	___	___	___
___	___	___	___
L	E	S	S

FOOL to WISE

F	O	O	L
_____	_____	_____	_____
_____	_____	_____	_____
_____	_____	_____	_____
_____	_____	_____	_____
_____	_____	_____	_____
W	I	S	E

GRUB to WORM

G	R	U	B
_____	_____	_____	_____
_____	_____	_____	_____
_____	_____	_____	_____
_____	_____	_____	_____
_____	_____	_____	_____
W	O	R	M

DAYS to YEAR

D	A	Y	S
____	____	____	____
____	____	____	____
____	____	____	____
____	____	____	____
____	____	____	____
Y	E	A	R

BORN to FREE

B	O	R	N
____	____	____	____
____	____	____	____
____	____	____	____
____	____	____	____
____	____	____	____
____	____	____	____
F	R	E	E

PAWN to KING

P	A	W	N
_____	_____	_____	_____
_____	_____	_____	_____
_____	_____	_____	_____
_____	_____	_____	_____
K	I	N	G

SEED to LAWN

S	E	E	D
_____	_____	_____	_____
_____	_____	_____	_____
_____	_____	_____	_____
_____	_____	_____	_____
L	A	W	N

HAND to FOOT

H	A	N	D
_____	_____	_____	_____
_____	_____	_____	_____

HAND to FOOT—continued

_____	_____	_____	_____
_____	_____	_____	_____
F	O	O	T

HEAT to FIRE

H	E	A	T
_____	_____	_____	_____
_____	_____	_____	_____
_____	_____	_____	_____
_____	_____	_____	_____
F	I	R	E

WORD to GAME

W	O	R	D
_____	_____	_____	_____
_____	_____	_____	_____
_____	_____	_____	_____
_____	_____	_____	_____
G	A	M	E

Five-Letter Word Ladders

Link these five-letter words together with a ladder of words. Each step in the ladder must be a real word, and must differ from the previous word by only one letter. There are many possible solutions, but try to use only the given number of steps. (Answers for this section begin on page 297.)

Example:

BLACK to WHITE

The answer is:

B	**L**	**A**	**C**	**K**
S	L	A	C	K
S	T	A	C	K
S	T	A	L	K
S	T	A	L	E
S	H	A	L	E
W	H	A	L	E
W	H	I	L	E
W	**H**	**I**	**T**	**E**

WHEAT to BREAD

This word ladder was given to the readers of *Vanity Fair* by Lewis Carroll.

W   H   E   A   T

___   ___   ___   ___   ___

___   ___   ___   ___   ___

___   ___   ___   ___   ___

___   ___   ___   ___   ___

B   R   E   A   D

SNACK to MEALS

S   N   A   C   K

___   ___   ___   ___   ___

___   ___   ___   ___   ___

___   ___   ___   ___   ___

___   ___   ___   ___   ___

M   E   A   L   S

FLESH to BLOOD

F	L	E	S	H
___	___	___	___	___
___	___	___	___	___
___	___	___	___	___
___	___	___	___	___
___	___	___	___	___
___	___	___	___	___
B	L	O	O	D

BABES to WOODS

B	A	B	E	S
___	___	___	___	___
___	___	___	___	___
___	___	___	___	___
___	___	___	___	___
W	O	O	D	S

NORTH to SOUTH

N	O	R	T	H
__	__	__	__	__
__	__	__	__	__
__	__	__	__	__
__	__	__	__	__
__	__	__	__	__
S	O	U	T	H

FRESH to STALE

F	R	E	S	H
__	__	__	__	__
__	__	__	__	__
__	__	__	__	__
__	__	__	__	__
__	__	__	__	__
__	__	__	__	__
S	T	A	L	E

SHARP to BLUNT

S   H   A   R   P

_____   _____   _____   _____   _____

_____   _____   _____   _____   _____

_____   _____   _____   _____   _____

_____   _____   _____   _____   _____

_____   _____   _____   _____   _____

_____   _____   _____   _____   _____

_____   _____   _____   _____   _____

B   L   U   N   T

TEARS to SMILE

T   E   A   R   S

_____   _____   _____   _____   _____

_____   _____   _____   _____   _____

_____   _____   _____   _____   _____

_____   _____   _____   _____   _____

_____   _____   _____   _____   _____

S   M   I   L   E

SMILE to FROWN

S	M	I	L	E
_____	_____	_____	_____	_____
_____	_____	_____	_____	_____
_____	_____	_____	_____	_____
_____	_____	_____	_____	_____
_____	_____	_____	_____	_____
_____	_____	_____	_____	_____
_____	_____	_____	_____	_____
F	R	O	W	N

SLEEP to DREAM

S	L	E	E	P
_____	_____	_____	_____	_____
_____	_____	_____	_____	_____
_____	_____	_____	_____	_____
_____	_____	_____	_____	_____
D	R	E	A	M

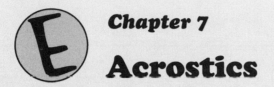

Chapter 7

Acrostics

An acrostic is a puzzle where the first letters of each line spell out a word. This kind of wordplay has been popular throughout history since before the time of Christ. Acrostics are a precursor to crossword puzzles, which are more popular but much younger, having been first created in 1913. This chapter has three different varieties of acrostic puzzles for your enjoyment.

Single Acrostics

For each puzzle, solve all of the clues, and the first letter of each solution will spell out another word. All of the words will be related to the theme in the title. (Answers for this section begin on page 297.)

Example:

Outside the Lines

1. Harvard nickname

2. Citrus

3. *The _____ Hill Mob*

4. Mediterranean oil tree

5. A communist

The answers are:

1. **C** rimson

2. **O** range

3. **L** avender

4. **O** live

5. **R** ed

The first letter of each answer spells out "**COLOR.**"

Reservations

1. Illegal parking note

2. It was less traveled

3. Flight business

4. Paid rest

5. A short journey

6. Sometimes lost on the way

May Flowers

1. To add salt and herbs

2. To place for growth

3. It pours

4. A creepy crawly

5. Never seen before

6. Vegetable plot

The Final Frontier

1. Found on Hollywood Boulevard

2. Mercury

3. Rocks in space

4. Halley's

5. UFO traveler

Beginning to Look a Lot Like

1. Roasting

2. Decked

3. Present decoration

4. Winter spike

5. Hung to be filled

6. Gift for the kids

7. Not even stirring

8. Heard on high

9. White dream

Earth Plot

1. Increase in size naturally

2. Edible tender young shoots

3. Pungent root vegetable

4. Move earth

5. Third planet from the sun

6. Mother

Baby

1. Not guilty

2. Brief sleep

3. Nourishment

4. We are not

5. Recent

6. Young child

Knowledge

1. A unit of instruction   _____

2. Process of gaining knowledge   _____

3. Reading, Writing, and   _____

4. Book activity   _____

5. Written records from class   _____

Athletics

1. Spectator place   _____

2. Makes perfect   _____

3. Racket stroke   _____

4. Competition for speed   _____

5. A running course   _____

6. A performance number   _____

Summer Fun

1. Area behind house

   _____

2. Before dust to dust

   _____

3. To ridicule harshly

   _____

4. Meat

   _____

5. To consume

   _____

6. Meal cooked and eaten outdoors

   _____

7. Dinner tools

   _____

8. A glowing coal

   _____

Double Acrostics

Solve all of the clues, and the first and last letter of each solution will spell out two more words. Only the two resulting words will be related to the theme in the title. (Answers for this section begin on page 297.)

Example:

Work and Play

The answer to this example first appeared in the *Magazine for the Young* in December 1854, "presented for the winter evening amusement of our young readers."

1. Drops from eye
2. Mined for iron
3. A storklike wading bird
4. A candle makes it

The answer is:

1. **T** e a **R**

2. **O** r **E**

3. **I** b i **S**

4. **L** i g h **T**

TOIL, REST

Sewing

1. Writer of fictional books

2. Tombstone text

3. Around the center of the earth

4. A challenge to prove courage

5. Second Bush First Lady

6. Received for services rendered

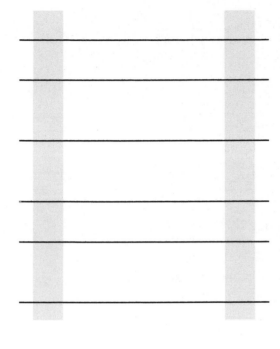

Wedding Bells

1. Making in an oven

2. One who publicly recites

3. Eskimo home

4. Dance club

5. Great excitement

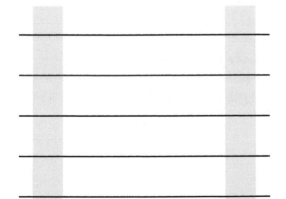

Assignment

1. The _____ and why _____

2. Central Florida tourist city _____

3. Chosen academic field
   of study _____

4. To set aside funds _____

Doing One Now

1. Feathered appendage _____

2. Vegetable used in gumbo _____

3. Order after scrambling _____

4. State the meaning _____

Four-Leaf Clover

1. Songlike style of poetry _____

2. Salt Lake state _____

3. Personal magnetism _____

4. Slang for mouth _____

5. Sweet potato _____

Defraud

1. Type of machine gun

   _____

2. Rough and ready

   _____

3. _____ State Building

   _____

4. South Pole

   _____

5. Court case

   _____

On the Silver Screen

1. Afternoon shows

   _____

2. Costume

   _____

3. Needed for overseas travel

   _____

4. Located inside

   _____

5. Leftovers

   _____

Cumulonimbus

1. At irregular intervals

   _____

2. Hot and humid

   _____

3. Smallest of the Great Lakes

   _____

Cumulonimbus—continued

4. French philosopher

5. Not extreme

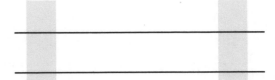

What a Racket

1. Facts of little importance

2. A public showing

3. Disgusting or filthy

4. Title character in popular underwater movie

5. He was an _____ to us all

6. Get dinner on the table

Composition

1. Russian physiologist with salivating dogs

2. Eight notes

3. Used to listen

4. Book submissions

5. Witty language that ridicules

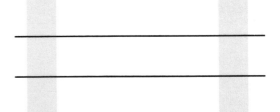

Acrostic Sayings

These puzzles have two parts. Solve all of the clues, then rearrange the solution words and add missing words to form a familiar saying. As an added bonus, the first letter of each solution will spell out a word that is related to the theme in the title. (Answers for this section begin on page 298.)

Example:

Rules of Conduct

1. More audible

2. Don't judge everyone from the _____ of a few

3. Made from letters

4. To utter

The answers are:

1. **L** ouder

2. **A** ctions

3. **W** ords

4. **S** peak

Actions speak louder than words.

** Bonus word**   **LAWS**

Captive

1. Lawn covering _____

2. Opposite of never _____

3. More inexperienced _____

4. The right or left part _____

_____

_____

** Bonus Word ** _____

Abbreviated Part of an Hour

1. A female parent _____

2. A new device, like from
   Edison _____

3. Something essential _____

_____

_____

** Bonus Word ** _____

Automatons Abbreviated

1. Pricked with teeth   _____

2. _____ upon a time   _____

3. Once more than once   _____

4. Wary of others   _____

_____

_____

** Bonus Word **   _____

Overnight Water

1. Letter starter   _____

2. A.K.A. grade school   _____

3. DNA scientist with Crick   _____

_____

_____

** Bonus Word **   _____

Auction Offer

1. Kick it when you die   _____

2. Not out   _____

3. A unit of rain   _____

_____

_____

*** Bonus Word ***   _____

Me and You

1. Between good and best   _____

2. One less than two   _____

3. One more than one   _____

4. Not tails   _____

_____

_____

*** Bonus Word ***   _____

Organized Crime Gang

1. Cycles from full to half and back _____

2. One time, no more _____

3. Sad color _____

_____

_____

** Bonus Word ** _____

Up-Down Toy

1. Second-person pronoun _____

2. If _____ you knew _____

3. Being in an early stage of life _____

4. Twice minus one _____

_____

_____

** Bonus Word ** _____

Auto

1. One who buys   _____

2. Forever and ever   _____

3. Might makes it   _____

_____

_____

** Bonus Word **   _____

Not Good

1. Cut with the teeth   _____

2. One more   _____

3. Vacuum cleaner eats it   _____

_____

_____

** Bonus Word **   _____

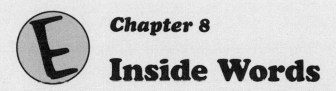

Chapter 8

Inside Words

What do you find when you dissect a word? Letters, of course, but also more words. The puzzles in this chapter require that you perform word surgery to see what is inside. So pick up your scalpel (which includes a cape, cap, and ape) and begin!

Charades

Charades was probably invented as a word game, not the acting game that is more familiar today. For this pencil-and-paper version of charades, first solve the clues to determine words. Then put the words together to form the final answer, which will be related to the title of the puzzle group. (Answers for this section begin on page 299.)

Example:

Gratified

1. Guilty or not guilty answer
2. Certain

The answer is plea+sure, or *pleasure*.

Buildings

1. High temperature
2. Short for elevated railway

_____ + _____ = _____

1. Chum
2. Single-spot card

_____ + _____ = _____

1. Switch position
2. Solid water

_____ + _____ = _____

At School

1. British snack
2. Bono partner

_____ + _____ = _____

1. Short for hello
2. A building floor

_____ + _____ = _____

1. Lower
2. Changed from off to _____

_____ + _____ = _____

Bird Watching

1. To take
2. Not out

_____ + _____ = _____

Bird Watching—continued

1. Bacon provider
2. A long, long time

_____ + _____ = _____

1. To practice boxing
2. Propel a boat

_____ + _____ = _____

In the Water

1. Between Sept. and Nov.
2. A numbered musical work

_____ + _____ = _____

1. He: she, his: _____
2. Finger circle

_____ + _____ = _____

In the Water—continued

1. Sixtieth of an hour abbreviated
2. Every _____ and then

_____ + _____ = _____

On the Land

1. A quick labored breath
2. Possessive form of she

_____ + _____ = _____

1. Organized crime leader
2. Opens doors

_____ + _____ = _____

1. Horse compartment in a barn
2. An atom with a charge

_____ + _____ = _____

Many Moods

1. Who _____ I?
2. Cheaper than new

_____ + _____ = _____

1. Argument against
2. Camping shelter

_____ + _____ = _____

1. Collectable piece of bric-a-brac
2. You, me, all of _____

_____ + _____ = _____

World Cities

1. Rotating piece mounted on a shaft
2. River crosser

_____ + _____ = _____

World Cities—continued

1. Fashionable

2. A long, long time _____

_____ + _____ = _____

1. Average golf score
2. What _____ the answer?

_____ + _____ = _____

Plants

1. Auto
2. A country

_____ + _____ = _____

1. A piece of land for a house
2. You + me = _____

_____ + _____ = _____

Plants—continued

1. _____ the people
2. Variety-show host Sullivan

_____ + _____ = _____

Around the House

1. Who _____ that masked man?
2. Partner of him

_____ + _____ = _____

1. Medicine swallowed whole
2. Ouch interjection

_____ + _____ = _____

1. Pie container
2. Try, _____ again

_____ + _____ = _____

Chicken Parts

1. An act of skill
2. _____ Majesty, the Queen

_____ + _____ = _____

1. _____ who is without sin
2. The product of creative activity

_____ + _____ = _____

1. Woman's undergarment worn for support
2. Opposite of out

_____ + _____ = _____

Containers

Solve each clue to determine two words. One of the words will be completely contained within the other word. (Answers for this section begin on page 299.)

Example:

"Money returned that contains a good time"

The answer is *refund* and *fun*.

U.S. Presidents

1. A president from Georgia who contains a creative work

   _____   _____

2. Early president who contains a tree

   _____   _____

3. Late-twentieth-century president who contains a bit of fluff

   _____   _____

Wildlife

1. An arachnid that contains approximately 3.14159

   _____   _____

2. A tasty crustacean that contains the edge of a basket

   _____   _____

3. A large aquatic reptile that contains a fish

   _____   _____

Vegetables

1. Slaw vegetable that contains a flexible container

   _____   _____

2. Green leafy vegetable that contains a bowling-ball target

   _____   _____

3. Tender green shoots that contain an average score

   _____   _____

Drink Up

1. Gin and dry vermouth that contains a malleable metal

   _____   _____

2. Sweet vermouth, whiskey, and a dash of bitters that contains head apparel

   _____   _____

3. Vodka and orange juice that contains a team of rowers

   _____   _____

Colors

1. Newspaper background color that contains a punch

   _____   _____

2. Chocolate color that contains a way to propel a boat

   _____   _____

3. Florida crop that contains what the telephone did

   _____   _____

Games

1. Card game that contains the Freudian source of instinctual demands

   _____   _____

2. Tile game that contains a negative

   _____   _____

3. Board game that contains a euphemism

   _____   _____

Dog Breeds

1. A fist fighter who contains a castrated bull

   _____   _____

2. A small hunting dog that contains the making of a mistake

   _____   _____

3. Wiener dog that contains a deliberate avoidance

   _____   _____

Plants

1. Lucky four leaf that contains a deep feeling of affection

   _____   _____

2. A holiday fruit that contains a baseball ref

   _____   _____

3. Yellow flower weed that contains a sandwich shop

   _____   _____

Careers

1. A small object built to scale that contains a lyric poem

   _____   _____

2. A chief that contains a knife wound

   _____   _____

3. An executive assistant that contains tobacco smoke residue

   _____   _____

Edible

1. Something roasted on sticks that contains a place for shopping

    _____   _____

2. Red fruit put on sandwiches that contains a flat pad

    _____   _____

3. Popular ice cream flavor that contains nothing

    _____   _____

 # *Ghosts*

In each puzzle you are given a sequence of three letters. Your task is to find at least three words that contain that sequence of letters in the order given. (Answers for this section begin on page 299.)

Example:

Sequence: **NVE**

Answers could include: co**nve**rt, **enve**lope, and i**nve**nt.

Sequence: **PST**

1. _____

2. _____

3. _____

Sequence: **NVA**

1. _____

2. _____

3. _____

Sequence: **YMN**

1. _____

2. _____

3. _____

Sequence: **NLA**

1. _____

2. _____

3. _____

Sequence: **THM**

1. _____

2. _____

3. _____

Sequence: **IZZ**

1. _____

2. _____

3. _____

Sequence: GGA

1. _____

2. _____

3. _____

Sequence: DUA

1. _____

2. _____

3. _____

Sequence: FFU

1. _____

2. _____

3. _____

Sequence: CKH

1. _____

2. _____

3. _____

Hidden Words

This is a game that was popular among the Victorians. The idea is to find words hidden within sentences. Your goal is to find three related words in each puzzle. (Answers for this section begin on page 300.)

Example:

Interesting Ashtray

A florid artsy pattern that includes a pink color adorns the latex ashtray.

> *The answers are:*
> 1. Florida
> 2. Colorado
> 3. Texas

A **[florid a]**rtsy pattern that includes a pink **[color ado]**rns the la**[tex as]**htray.

Beware of Liposuction

A Timbuktu liposuction can cause asthma. Plenty of people in Genoa know this already.

1. _____

2. _____

3. _____

Stuntman

As the car rotated rapidly, the spin achieved Jimmy a spot atop the daredevil hall of fame.

1. _____

2. _____

3. _____

Food Fit

He threw a tantrum, petrified that the tub actually contained ravioli noodles.

1. _____

2. _____

3. _____

Whirlwind

She watched the tornado grab bits of the replica that were loose.

1. _____

2. _____

3. _____

Problem Child

Lisa turns away even us. She only talks to her friends in grammar school.

1. _____

2. _____

3. _____

First Names

In the following puzzles see what you can make of some common first names. Solve the clues with words that contain the given first name. (Answers for this section begin on page 301.)

Example:

Chuck

1. A hole in the road
2. A rock-dwelling lizard
3. To vomit

The answers are:
1. Chuckhole
2. Chuckwalla
3. Upchuck

Bob

1. A small lynx

   _____

2. A British policeman

   _____

3. Shorter posterior part

   _____

4. Worn from the ankle to the toe

   _____

5. For snow racing

   _____

Jack

1. A big award   _____

2. Pancake   _____

3. Vehicle seizure   _____

4. A person who fells trees   _____

Tom

1. A boyish girl   _____

2. A male cat   _____

3. A person without good judgment   _____

4. Native American ax   _____

Mary

1. Preliminary election   _____

2. One of the original thirteen colonies   _____

3. Seasoning   _____

4. In accordance with convention   _____

Jim

1. Excellent of its kind   _____

2. A short crowbar   _____

3. Poisonous tropical weed   _____

4. Sprinkled on ice cream   _____

Bill

1. A pocket-size case for money   _____

2. A person from a backwoods area _____

3. An advertisement   _____

4. A male goat   _____

5. A theatrical program   _____

Chapter 9

Missing Pieces

In this information age, words are often shortened so that more material can be packed into a single message. For example, maybe you already know that LOL is "laughing out loud" and AKA is "also known as." But the puzzles in this chapter take this idea to an extreme and test your skill at understanding messages with a lot of missing pieces.

Abbreviated Sayings

Some of the words in the common sayings in this section have been replaced with their first letters. Your challenge is to determine the complete phrase for each saying. (Answers for this section begin on page 301.)

Example:

Sound Advice

1. Do U O as they W D U you.

2. W there's S, there's F.

3. L before you L.

The answers are:

1. Do unto others as they would do unto you.

2. Where there's smoke, there's fire.

3. Look before you leap.

For the Birds

1. A B in the H is W 2 in the B.

   _____

2. K 2 B with 1 S.

   _____

3. The E B C the W.

   _____

Equestrian

1. I'm so H I could E a H.

   _____

2. Don't P the C B the H

   _____

3. You can L a H to W, but you C M him D.

   _____

Time

1. T and T W for no M.

   _____

2. T H all W.

   _____

3. A S in T S 9.

   _____

In the Family

1. Like F, like S. _____

2. B is T than W. _____

3. N is the M of I. _____

Career Advice

1. All W and no P M J a D B. _____

2. Nothing V, N G. _____

3. If at F you don't S, T, T A. _____

Love Advice

1. A makes the H G F. _____

2. It T 2 to T. _____

3. B is in the E of the B. _____

Landscape

1. The C is A G on the O S of the F. _____

2. A R S gathers no M. _____

3. M a M out of a M. _____

Timely Advice

1. B L than N. _____

2. N put off U T what Y C D T. _____

3. S while the I is H. _____

Poultry

1. Don't C your C B they H. _____

2. B of a F F together. _____

3. Don't put A your E in 1 B. _____

In the Kitchen

1. Too many C S the B. _____

2. O of the F P into the F. _____

3. If you C S the H, get O of the K. _____

Lacking

1. A F in N is a F I. _____

2. B can't be C. _____

3. F keepers, L W. _____

Nature

1. S W run D. _____

2. When the C A, the M will P. _____

3. You R what Y S. _____

Words

1. One P is W a T W.

2. A speak L than W.

3. A W to the W.

Wheel Around

1. The S W gets the G.

2. What goes A C A.

3. Don't P the C before the H.

Force

1. U we S, D we F.

2. M makes R.

3. F R in where A F to T.

Abbreviated Cinema

In the following puzzles, movie titles and their stars have been abbreviated to initial letters only. Your challenge is to determine the movie title, with extra credit if you can get all of the stars. To make things easier, popular movies have been chosen and their year of release is given. (Answers for this section begin on page 302.)

Example:
Movie: **T M** (1999)
Starring:

- K R

- L F

The answer is:
The Matrix, starring Keanu Reeves and Laurence Fishburne.

Abbreviated Cinema Challenge 1

Movie: **F G** (1994) _____
Starring:

- T H _____

- R W P _____

- G S _____

Abbreviated Cinema Challenge 2

Movie: **T** (1997)   _____
Starring:

- L D   _____

- K W   _____

Abbreviated Cinema Challenge 3

Movie: **P F** (1994)   _____
Starring:

- J T   _____

- S L J   _____

- U T   _____

Abbreviated Cinema Challenge 4

Movie: **R O T L A** (1981)   _____
Starring:

- H F   _____

- K A   _____

- P F   _____

Abbreviated Cinema Challenge 5

Movie: **A N** (1979) _____

Starring:

- M B _____

- R D _____

- M S _____

Abbreviated Cinema Challenge 6

Movie: **S W** (1977) _____

Starring:

- M H _____

- II F _____

- C F _____

- A G _____

Abbreviated Cinema Challenge 7

Movie: **T D** (1976)   _____

Starring:

- R D N   _____

- C S   _____

- J F   _____

- H K   _____

Abbreviated Cinema Challenge 8

Movie: **T G** (1972)   _____

Starring:

- M B   _____

- A P   _____

- J C   _____

- R D   _____

Abbreviated Cinema Challenge 9

Movie: **T K A M** (1962) _____

Starring:

- G P _____

- R D _____

- B P _____

Abbreviated Cinema Challenge 10

Movie: **S I T R** (1952) _____
Starring:

- G K _____

- D O _____

- D R _____

Abbreviated Cinema Challenge 11

Movie: **I A W L** (1946) _____
Starring:

- J S _____

- D R _____

- L B _____

Abbreviated Cinema Challenge 12

Movie: **C** (1942) _____

Starring:

- H B _____

- I B _____

Abbreviated Cinema Challenge 13

Movie: **C K** (1941) _____

Starring:

- U W _____

- J C _____

Abbreviated Cinema Challenge 14

Movie: **G W T W** (1939) _____

Starring:

- V L _____

- C G _____

Formulaics

Here is a challenge that is all about equality. Each of these puzzles involves a simple equation. Here's the twist: the numbers are all there, but each word has been substituted with its initial letter. (Answers for this section begin on page 302.)

Example:

Solve this equation: 24 H = 1 D.

The answer is 24 Hours = 1 Day.

Red, White, and Blue

- 50 S = USA   _____

- G L = S + H + E + O + M   _____

- 13 O C = M + R I + C + N H + N Y + D + N J + P + V + M + N C + S C + G

  _____

Lists

- N + S + E + W = C P   _____

- J + P + G + R = B (hint: British)   _____

- U + O + I + E + A = V   _____

Story Time

- $7 D = G + D + B + S + S + H + D$

_____

- $S R = D + D + P + V + C + C + D + B$

_____

- $3 B = M B + P B + B B$

_____

Sports

- $100 Y = 1 F F$

_____

- $52 C = 1 D$

_____

- $18 H = 1 G C$

_____

For Good Measure

- $12 I = 1 F$

_____

- $360 D = 1 C$

_____

- $3 F = 1 Y$

_____

Color and Composition

- $1 P = 1,000 W$

_____

- $B + R + Y = P C$

_____

- $1 S = 4 S$

_____

Time

- 7 D = 1 W

  _____

- 12 M = 1 Y

  _____

- M + T + W + T + F = W

  _____

Makes Sense

- 100 C = 1 D

  _____

- P S = P E

  _____

- 2 Q + 3 N = 65 P

  _____

Chapter 10

Triplets

A lot of new dictionary entries are simply old words that have been combined together. For example, *online, age-old,* and even *mommy track* have all found their way into most dictionaries. This chapter tests your skill at determining these kinds of compound words that occur in groups of three.

Around the House Triplets

In each of the following puzzles, determine the common word that can be combined with each of the three given words. As a bonus, the puzzle's title will give you a clue to a fourth compound word. (Answers for this section begin on page 303.)

Note: Remember, compounds can be open (*high school*), closed (*preschool)* or hyphenated (*school-aged*).

Example:

Wipe Your Feet

1. trap

2. prize

3. out

The common word is *door,* which makes the answers *trapdoor, door prize,* and *outdoor.*

The word for the puzzle's title is *doormat.*

Within the Mattress

1. chicken _____

2. off _____

3. board _____

Sewage Disposal

1. gas _____

2. top _____

3. think _____

School Assignment

1. made _____

2. nursing _____

3. spun _____

Elevated Fort

1. Christmas _____

2. top _____

3. hugger _____

Dust Guard

1. pink _____

2. knot _____

3. stream _____

Hourglass

1. goose _____

2. white _____

3. head _____

Outdoors Triplets

Find the common word that can be combined with each of the three given words. As a bonus, the puzzle's title will give you a clue to a fourth compound word. An example is given at the start of this chapter. (Answers for this section begin on page 303.)

Light in Flight

1. ball _____

2. butter _____

3. dragon _____

A Plant with Edible Fruit

1. grass _____

2. baby _____

3. bird _____

Ocean Boundary

1. dead _____

2. man _____

3. hair _____

An Overwhelming Victory

1. heart _____

2. lord _____

3. main _____

Farm Fence with a Twist

1. hay _____

2. service _____

3. hot _____

A Speedy Bird

1. rail _____

2. rage _____

3. kill _____

Sports Triplets

Find the common word that can be combined with each of the three given words. As a bonus, the puzzle's title will give you a clue to a fourth compound word. An example is given at the start of this chapter. (Answers for this section begin on page 303.)

Football Helmet Front

1. bold _____

2. poker _____

3. card _____

Boxing Victory

1. down _____

2. knee _____

3. off _____

Heavy Metal Toss

1. big _____

2. gun _____

3. long _____

Race Refueling

1. gap _____

2. watch _____

3. short _____

Hoops

1. moth _____

2. point _____

3. room _____

Football Leader

1. draw _____

2. space _____

3. horse _____

Media Triplets

Find the common word that can be combined with each of the three given words. As a bonus, the puzzle's title will give you a clue to a fourth compound word. An example is given at the start of this chapter. (Answers for this section begin on page 303.)

Rouse the Troops

1. show _____

2. sweet _____

3. shop _____

Info Delivered to Your Door

1. back _____

2. sand _____

3. thin _____

Internet Maintainer

1. mind _____

2. grand _____

3. piece _____

TV Forecaster

1. vane _____

2. fair _____

3. proof _____

TV—with Prizes

1. word _____

2. fair _____

3. plan _____

Strictly Business Triplets

Find the common word that can be combined with each of the three given words. As a bonus, the puzzle's title will give you a clue to a fourth compound word. An example is given at the start of this chapter. (Answers for this section begin on page 303.)

Price Reduction

1. hall   _____

2. post   _____

3. book   _____

Farmer's Tool

1. sales   _____

2. dark   _____

3. fever   _____

Paper Money

1. foot   _____

2. book   _____

3. key   _____

The Presiding Officer

1. lift   _____

2. high   _____

3. arm   _____

Greeting or Agreement

1. milk   _____

2. down   _____

3. up   _____

Office Pen

1. check   _____

2. needle   _____

3. blank   _____

Eat and Drink Triplets

Find the common word that can be combined with each of the three given words. As a bonus, the puzzle's title will give you a clue to a fourth compound word. An example is given at the start of this chapter. (Answers for this section begin on page 304.)

County Fair Fare

1. top _____

2. house _____

3. tag _____

A Common Quantity of Beer

1. horse _____

2. back _____

3. fanny _____

Illegal Whiskey

1. blue _____

2. honey _____

3. struck _____

After Heavy Drinking

1. cast _____

2. once _____

3. drive _____

Occupations Triplets

Find the common word that can be combined with each of the three given words. As a bonus, the puzzle's title will give you a clue to a fourth compound word. An example is given at the start of this chapter. (Answers for this section begin on page 304.)

Pool Protector

1. still _____

2. style _____

3. wild _____

Man in the Armed Forces

1. answering _____

2. secret _____

3. charge _____

Mechanic

1. bars _____

2. business _____

3. wrench _____

Movie Author

1. smoke _____

2. sun _____

3. silk _____

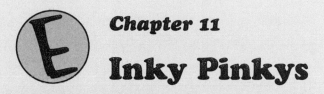

Chapter 11

Inky Pinkys

Why do people like rhymes so much? Perhaps it is because the musical sound of rhymes adds to their meaning, and helps convey emotion. Rhymes are used in poetry, speeches, and songs to add a dimension plain prose does not have, something that takes the listener to another level of understanding. But, as you will find out in this chapter, one simple reason to like rhymes is because they are fun!

Single-Syllable Rhymes

Based on the given clues, determine pairs of single-syllable words that rhyme. (Answers for this section begin on page 304.)

Example:

1. Baseball referee hop

2. An informal conversation with a rodent

The answers are:

1. ump jump

2. rat chat

Animals

1. A dull sideways crustacean   _____

2. A boy marine mammal   _____

3. A gorilla's shoulder garment   _____

All Wet

1. Spot caused from precipitation   _____

2. Large body of water with vipers   _____

3. A moist tent city   _____

This and That

1. 365-day hearing organ

   _____

2. Creek read cover to cover

   _____

3. Polite request for a small round vegetable

   _____

Yummy

1. A sugary, special delight

   _____

2. Between-meal food hut

   _____

3. A false birthday dessert

   _____

Mammals

1. An uncommon female horse

   _____

2. Grizzly fur filaments

   _____

3. Inexpensive wooly mammal

   _____

Hygiene

1. A well-washed person, thirteen to nineteen

   _____

2. Unusual facial hair

   _____

3. A route to the tub

   _____

Wildlife

1. Jaws playground _____

2. No-charge honey insect _____

3. An overweight feline _____

Nonverbal Communication

1. 50 percent ha ha _____

2. A courageous hello hand gesture _____

3. A brief kiss between the head and shoulders _____

Work

1. Compensated house cleaner _____

2. Paycheck anger _____

3. Intellectual labor down the sink _____

Transportation

1. Competition to the moon _____

2. Famous performer vehicle _____

3. A big, flat-bottomed freight boat _____

Sports

1. A hut by a running course

_____

2. An exceptionally good group of athletes on the same side

_____

3. A little sphere

_____

Includes an S Word

1. A road that runs quickly

_____

2. An intelligent beginning

_____

3. Sodium chloride storage chamber

_____

Around the House

1. A carrier for Old Glory

_____

2. Displays a picture of a girl

_____

3. An extra piece of furniture to sit on

_____

Animal Life

1. A nuisance in a bird's home

_____

2. Rodent's game cube

_____

3. A fast young chicken

_____

Things People Do

1. A quick stealer _____

2. Animal park gang of workers _____

3. Security person for the area around a house _____

Apparel

1. Mud on your blouse _____

2. Garment worn while playing game with
    kings and queens _____

3. A thin head covering _____

Colorful Food

1. Light brown cereal _____

2. Unripe lima _____

3. Primary-color beer _____

Odds and Ends

1. A crimson cord _____

2. A really nice ringer _____

3. A fat twig _____

Shopping

1. A tiny shopping complex

   _____

2. A rapid present

   _____

3. Purchase of a round, filled pastry

   _____

Body Functions

1. A sound slumber

   _____

2. Hearing-organ phobia

   _____

3. Alpine smooch

   _____

Family

1. A happy father

   _____

2. Uncivilized young person

   _____

3. Home for a rodent family

   _____

Manmade

1. A soaked 747

   _____

2. A large excavation

   _____

3. A conceited railroad car

   _____

Small Change

1. A ten-cent unlawful activity

   _____

2. Coin holder for a hospital caregiver

   _____

3. A pleasing cost for purchase

   _____

 # Double-Syllable Rhymes

Based on the given clues, determine pairs of double-syllable words that rhyme. (Answers for this section begin on page 305.)

Example:
Jabbering from a baseball player

The answer is _batter chatter._

The Great Outdoors

1. A spring of water on Everest

   _____

2. A flower provider in the deep woods

   _____

3. An amazing noise after lightning

   _____

Anthropomorphize

1. A smarter Old Faithful hot spring

2. A four-legged reptile sorcerer

3. A humorous and clever cat

Sports World

1. Puck sport played by horse riders

2. Personal goods compartment for a kicking game

3. Thrower for a baseball team with more money

B Word Included

1. Superior knit pullover

2. A fatter car protector

3. Sickness of dam-building rodents

Odd Occupations

1. Pipe repairperson who works between spring and autumn

   _____

2. Rainwater trough trimmer

   _____

3. A teacher of how to ride a skateboard with a handle

   _____

Personal Descriptions

1. A sleepy person who does not win

   _____

2. One who acquires car wheels

   _____

3. A better dinner eater

   _____

By the Numbers

1. Tiny finger, toe, or number

   _____

2. Five-cent prepared cucumber

   _____

3. Unwashed between twenty-nine and thirty-one

   _____

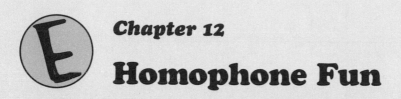

Chapter 12

Homophone Fun

Homophones are words that have the same pronunciation but are spelled differently and have different meanings. (For example: pair, pear, and pare.) Don't confuse them with homographs, which are words that are spelled the same but have different meanings (the *bow* on a gift, or the *bow* on a boat). Homophones can often lead to confusion and misunderstanding, which is why they are so much fun!

Homophone Pairs

From the clues, determine pairs of words that have the same pronunciation but are spelled differently and have different meanings. (Answers for this section begin on page 305.)

Example
A penny perfume

The answer is *cent scent*.

Homophone Pair Challenge 1

1. Forbidden group of musicians

   _____

2. A rough-sounding stallion

   _____

3. Glare at the steps

   _____

Homophone Pair Challenge 2

1. A special deal on boat cloth

   _____

2. Lacking strength Sunday through Saturday

   _____

3. Opportune moment for this seasoning

   _____

Homophone Pair Challenge 3

1. A frog pulled by a chain

   _____

2. An honest price paid for transit

   _____

3. Posters of male royalty

   _____

Homophone Pair Challenge 4

1. Sell a bike foot part _____

2. A chess horse after dark _____

3. Much-loved hoofed mammal _____

Homophone Pair Challenge 5

1. An unemployed movie star with a devoted following _____

2. Insect's parent's sister _____

3. A sorrowful dawn _____

Homophone Pair Challenge 6

1. A raw metal rowing pole _____

2. To compose correctly _____

3. A rough path _____

Homophone Pair Challenge 7

1. A lion's primary hair _____

2. To cure the back part of the foot _____

3. A pleasing hotel space with multiple rooms _____

Homophone Pair Challenge 8

1. Orange vegetable gold measure   _____

2. One with meals and lodging on the edge   _____

3. Shivering meat and bean stew   _____

Homophone Pair Challenge 9

1. Money made from one who is divinely inspired _____

2. Earth's star's offspring   _____

3. An up-to-date edible berry   _____

Homophone Pair Challenge 10

1. A light-colored bucket   _____

2. A foot digit pull   _____

3. A synagogue singer riding pace   _____

Homophone Pair Challenge 11

1. A painful glide   _____

2. A dull wood plank   _____

3. A marine mammal cry   _____

Homophone Pair Challenge 12

1. A fermented grape juice cry

    _____

2. A sequence of breakfast food in a box

    _____

3. A solitary sum borrowed from the bank

    _____

Homophone Pair Challenge 13

1. Take this metal alloy

    _____

2. Apparel worn to shut down

    _____

3. Naked grizzly

    _____

Homophone Pair Challenge 14

1. Nervous canvas shelters

    _____

2. A group of animals that are listened to

    _____

3. An offensive chicken

    _____

Homophone Pair Challenge 15

1. Money hidden in a safe place

    _____

2. An introduction to animal flesh

    _____

3. A more courageous large rock

    _____

Homophone Pair Challenge 16

1. An antagonistic but cheap inn

    _____

2. A corn puzzle

    _____

3. An underaged ore digger

    _____

Homophone Pair Challenge 17

1. Completely divine

    _____

2. Rabbit fur

    _____

3. A contract provision regarding sharp
   fingernails

    _____

Homophone Pair Challenge 18

1. An entire cavity

    _____

2. Boy letters

    _____

3. A government fee on these short nails

    _____

Homophone Pair Challenge 19

1. A representation of a brass percussive instrument

   _____

2. To chop this after-dinner candy into small pieces

   _____

3. Horse wedding harness

   _____

Homophone Pair Challenge 20

1. Basement peddler

   _____

2. A superior gambler

   _____

3. One who sows these pine trees

   _____

Sounds Similar

Determine the original words that sound similar to the given words. Note that these words are not perfect homophones. Some people find it helpful to read the puzzles out loud to hear what they sound like. (Answers for this section begin on page 306.)

Example:

Famous Plays

1. As treat corn aimed ease ire
2. Row me own July it
3. Day crew Sybil

The answers are:

1. *A Streetcar Named Desire*
2. *Romeo and Juliet*
3. *The Crucible*

Basketball

1. Caramel own _____

2. Lare repaired _____

3. Filch hacks on _____

Trees

1. Pie hen _____

2. May pole _____

3. See dare _____

United

1. Can sass   _____

2. My shogun   _____

3. Numb hex ago   _____

Fine Wine

1. Bar candy   _____

2. Cobb ernie   _____

3. Chaired any   _____

Authors

1. Ad growling pole   _____

2. Market Wang   _____

3. Stay finking   _____

Reptiles

1. A leg at her   _____

2. Lies hard   _____

3. Cameo lawn   _____

Stars

1. Dead lemur _____

2. Launch any _____

3. Marry lineman row _____

Birds

1. Hair in _____

2. Car Daniel _____

3. Egg hill _____

Movies

1. Lie inking _____

2. Sway tome hallow beam a _____

3. Hoe chin's sell oven _____

Television

1. Chip party _____

2. Hall midge hill drain _____

3. Frays cheer _____

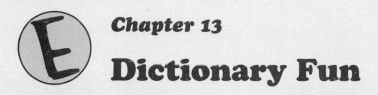

Chapter 13

Dictionary Fun

If you've read the dictionary from cover to cover, then you'll do really well with the challenges in this chapter. On the other hand, don't worry if you haven't. A love of words is all that is required to have fun with these puzzles. Get ready to test your knowledge of information found in the dictionary.

Spelling Bee

The spelling bee was reportedly started in New England in the 1870s and quickly became very popular. In this pencil-and-paper version, your challenge is to find and correct the one misspelling in each set of four words. (Answers for this section begin on page 306.)

Example:

- mathematics
- embarrass
- millenium
- deterrence

The answer is *millennium*.

Spelling Challenge 1

- missile
- acquire
- pursue
- accidentaly ✓

Spelling Challenge 2

- genius
- seize
- weird
- manuever ✓

Spelling Challenge 3

- seperate ✓
- argument
- deceive
- similar

Spelling Challenge 4

- acquaintance
- simile
- undoubtedly
- potatoe ✓

Spelling Challenge 5

- prejudice
- absence
- camoflage ✓
- business

Spelling Challenge 6

- necessary
- parallel
- definate ✓
- formerly

Spelling Challenge 7

- handkerchief
- desperate
- bargan ✓
- government

Spelling Challenge 8

- embarrassment
- occured ✓
- tragedy
- mischievous

Spelling Challenge 9

- vilage ✓
- performance
- colonel
- siege

Spelling Challenge 10

- suprise ✓
- sacrilegious
- grammar
- immediately

Spelling Challenge 11

- marriage
- irresistible
- generaly ✓
- accordion

Spelling Challenge 12

- permissible
- cemetary ✓
- especially
- rhythm

Spelling Challenge 13

- fiery
- incredible
- believe
- existance ✓

Spelling Challenge 14

- knowledge
- salary
- occurrence
- accomodate ✓

Spelling Challenge 15

- humorus ✓
- receipt
- explanation
- ridiculous

Spelling Challenge 16

- ecstasy
- incidentally
- pronounciation ✓
- proceed

Spelling Challenge 17

- hypocrisy
- repetition
- occassion ✓
- indispensable

Spelling Challenge 18

- recomend ✓
- defendant
- privilege
- miniscule

Spelling Challenge 19

- lieutenant
- accumulate
- disapoint ✓
- criticize

Spelling Challenge 20

- begining ✓
- sergeant
- receive
- barbecue

The Age of Words

The dictionary was not always as thick as it is today. New words are continually being added as inventions are created and our culture changes. Every new development calls for a new word to describe it. Can you tell how long words have been around? Sort the three words in each group from oldest to newest. (Answers for this section begin on page 307.)

Example:
- touch
- glob
- ape

The correct order from oldest to newest is:
1. ape
2. touch
3. glob

Age of Words Challenge 1

_____ antenna
_____ kettle
_____ tent

Age of Words Challenge 2

_____ phony
_____ voyage
_____ candle

Age of Words Challenge 3

_____ dish
_____ voyeur
_____ narcotic

Age of Words Challenge 4

_____ aquifer
_____ play
_____ suit

Age of Words Challenge 5

_____ prune
_____ barrette
_____ dwarf

Age of Words Challenge 6

_____ stride
_____ calibrator
_____ abstain

Age of Words Challenge 7

_____ ethanol
_____ toothache
_____ greet

Age of Words Challenge 8

_____ antilog
_____ chemistry
_____ key

Age of Words Challenge 9

_____ wrangle
_____ nifty
_____ yellow

Age of Words Challenge 10

_____ freeze
_____ escalator
_____ iron

Age of Words Challenge 11

_____ warrior
_____ malnourished
_____ tough

Age of Words Challenge 12

_____ antonym
_____ half
_____ alley

Age of Words Challenge 13

_____ nosedive
_____ tide
_____ princess

Age of Words Challenge 14

_____ mindset
_____ pamper
_____ flea

Age of Words Challenge 15

_____ meridian
_____ thief
_____ agnostic

Age of Words Challenge 16

_____ wonder
_____ tendinitis
_____ windmill

Age of Words Challenge 17

_____ gold
_____ malarkey
_____ gag

Age of Words Challenge 18

_____ spoonerism
_____ hook
_____ vengeance

Age of Words Challenge 19

_____ hat
_____ internment
_____ adulation

Age of Words Challenge 20

_____ verdict
_____ amputee
_____ birch

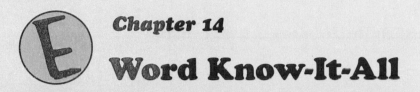

Chapter 14

Word Know-It-All

Words are fun, but they are also powerful. Knowing the right word at the right time can often make the crucial difference in communicating with others. Thus, a larger vocabulary could change your life! Complete the puzzles in this chapter and you will be on your way to becoming a word know-it-all.

Easier Words

Select the best definition for a word from the three choices. (Answers for this section begin on page 307.)

Example:

Pick the best definition for Antagonism

a. Hostility
b. Small animal with eight legs
c. Disorder characterized by difficulty in breathing

The answer is *hostility.*

Pick the Best Definition for Allied

a. Related
b. Primitive in culture and customs
c. A purple gemstone

Pick the Best Definition for Armistice

a. To obtain by foraging
b. A truce
c. A disease caused by a lack of vitamin C

Pick the Best Definition for Disbar

a. To expel from the legal profession
b. A male turkey
c. Transitory

Pick the Best Definition for Truant

a. A student who stays away from school without permission
b. Having power to review decisions
c. The rear opening of the alimentary canal

Pick the Best Definition for
Lye

  a. A person having both extrovert and introvert characteristics
  ✓b. A strong alkaline substance used in making soap
  c. Inflammation of joints

Pick the Best Definition for
Nip

  a. Removed or distant
  b. The part of the anchor that hooks the ground
  ✓c. A small amount of liquor

Pick the Best Definition for
Aperture

  a. Monotonous
  b. A handrail
  ✓c. An opening

Pick the Best Definition for
Mediate

  a. A long boat used on the canals in Venice, Italy
  b. To expel from the legal profession
  ✓c. To settle differences between conflicting parties

Pick the Best Definition for
Assent

  a. Routine carried out mechanically
  b. Portion of the atmosphere from twenty to fifty miles above the earth
  ✓c. Consent

Pick the Best Definition for
Disparage

  a. Impose a fine
  ✓b. To degrade
  c. Something abnormal or unusual

Pick the Best Definition for
Barbiturate

  ✓a. A group of drugs that act as depressants
  b. Word made by rearranging the letters of another word
  c. A blade attached to the muzzle of a rifle

Pick the Best Definition for
Altercation

  ✓a. A noisy, angry dispute
  b. Self-government
  c. To make impure by adding things

Pick the Best Definition for
Amphetamine

   a. Lack of government or order

  ✓b. Drug used as a stimulant

   c. Struck with horror

Pick the Best Definition for
Aggregate

  ✓a. Total amount

   b. Word of opposite meaning

   c. The study of excrement

Pick the Best Definition for
Flit

   a. Main artery leading from the heart

   b. Shapeless

  ✓c. To pass abruptly

Pick the Best Definition for
Ampere

   a. A wise and trusted counselor

   b. Ability to make responsible decisions

  ✓c. Unit of electric current

Pick the Best Definition for
Mesosphere

  ✓a. Portion of the atmosphere from twenty to fifty miles above the earth

   b. Shameless

   c. Red-brown color

Pick the Best Definition for
Au gratin

  ✓a. With a cheese crust

   b. Fish eggs

   c. Slowly

Pick the Best Definition for
Anterior

   a. Ease

   b. A Middle Eastern paste made with chickpeas

  ✓c. Located before in place or time

Pick the Best Definition for
Alibi

   a. To divest of corporeal existence

   b. Aid given to help the poor

  ✓c. An excuse

Pick the Best Definition for Bayou

   a. To strip of money or property by fraud

✓b. A marshy inlet

   c. One that is inexperienced

Pick the Best Definition for Jaundice

   a. Quick and nimble

   b. Skillful and clever

✓c. Disorder with the symptom of yellowish skin

Pick the Best Definition for Alpha

✓a. First letter in the Greek alphabet

   b. Obviously offensive

   c. To put together carelessly

Pick the Best Definition for Transcribe

✓a. To make a written copy of

   b. A difficult position

   c. To cause to awaken

Pick the Best Definition for Avail

   a. The average value of a set of numbers

✓b. To be of use

   c. Science of crop production

Pick the Best Definition for Writhe

   a. Person who fraudulently pretends to have knowledge in a field

   b. Near

✓ c. To twist and turn the body

Pick the Best Definition for Plague

   a. A long, adventurous journey

   b. Disorder with the symptom of yellowish skin

✓c. Pestilence

Pick the Best Definition for Avow

   a. A writer

   b. Branched horn of a deer

✓c. Declare openly

Harder Words

Select the best definition for a word from the three choices. (Answers for this section begin on page 308.)

Pick the Best Definition for Avoirdupois

✓ a. System of weight measurement

b. Room leading to another room

c. To warm oneself

Pick the Best Definition for Scaphoid

a. Sea creature with the head of a man and the tail of a fish

b. Painfully difficult work

c. Shaped like a boat

Pick the Best Definition for Atomizer

✓ a. Device for spraying liquid as a mist

b. An ancient commentator on the classics

c. A discharge from a debt or obligation

Pick the Best Definition for Mesopause

a. Berrylike

b. Unite

c. Atmospheric area about fifty miles above the earth's surface

Pick the Best Definition for Alveolate

✓ a. Pitted like a honeycomb

b. Bristly fibers on a head of barley

c. Melancholy

Pick the Best Definition for Quartan

a. Occurring every fourth day

b. A grotesque doll or person

c. Not eating or drinking too much

Pick the Best Definition for Babushka

a. Thinking

b. A type of scarf

c. Needle-shaped

Pick the Best Definition for Flout

a. Throwback

b. To scorn or scoff

c. Middle

Pick the Best Definition for Quindecennial

a. A curved single-edged Asian sword

b. A fifteenth anniversary

c. Existing before the U.S. Civil War

Pick the Best Definition for Cerement

a. Occurring every fourth day

b. Quiet

c. A burial garment

Pick the Best Definition for Agora

a. A gathering place

b. Behind in payment

c. A church announcement of an upcoming marriage

Pick the Best Definition for Cespitose

a. A flat bread usually made with oatmeal or barley flour

b. Climbing

c. Growing in clumps, like moss

Pick the Best Definition for Platitude

a. A precious metal

b. A trite remark

c. To slander

Pick the Best Definition for Quadruped

a. An animal with four feet

b. Starchy

c. To translate literally

Pick the Best Definition for
Distend

a. To become expanded

b. Capable of acting as an acid or a base

c. To cut across

Pick the Best Definition for
Zizith

a. A hunter

b. The tassels worn on traditional garments by Jewish males

c. Food of the gods

Pick the Best Definition for
Anthracite

a. A tryst

b. Hard coal

c. The innermost sanctuary in a temple

Pick the Best Definition for
Quadrille

a. Adjunct or accessory

b. A dance of French origin

c. A church announcement of an upcoming marriage

Pick the Best Definition for
Gouache

a. A mechanical device for controlling something

b. A technique of painting using opaque watercolors

c. A hunter

Pick the Best Definition for
Placate

a. Medium-sized tubular pasta

b. To lessen

c. To appease

Pick the Best Definition for
Baba

a. Ambush

b. A rum cake usually made with raisins

c. A long monotonous discourse

Pick the Best Definition for
Anabiosis

a. To flee and hide

b. Toward the stern

c. Moving again after apparent death

Pick the Best Definition for Ampoule

a. Container for a dose of medicine

b. A vivid purplish red color

c. Harmonious

Pick the Best Definition for Jackanapes

a. A mischievous child

b. Starch from a tropical plant root

c. Agreeableness

Pick the Best Definition for Asperity

a. Foul-mouthed

b. Either of a pair of metal stands for logs

c. Harshness

Pick the Best Definition for Soliloquy

a. Strong brown wrapping paper

b. Talking to oneself

c. Washing of the body

Pick the Best Definition for Abaft

a. A soldier's belt that is worn across the chest

b. A keyboard instrument that produces bell-like tones

c. Toward the stern

Pick the Best Definition for Rondo

a. Lazy eye

b. A musical form in which a refrain recurs four times

c. Foretell

Pick the Best Definition for Acephalous

a. Without a head

b. A genus of plant with cup-shaped flowers

c. Defender of a doctrine

Pick the Best Definition for Jato

a. An aircraft takeoff assisted by an auxiliary jet

b. A barrel organ

c. First letter of the Hebrew alphabet

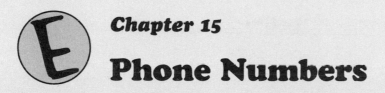

Chapter 15

Phone Numbers

The first two digits of a phone number used to be an abbreviation of the local exchange name. Even today many companies will advertise their phone numbers as letters or words, and all phone dials include both letters and numbers. The puzzles in this chapter test your skill at decoding words found in phone numbers.

Five-Digit Numbers

Decode the digits to come up with five-letter words for each category. You are given the digits that are coded as on most telephones:

1	**4 = GHI**	**7 = PRS**
2 = ABC	**5 = JKL**	**8 = TUV**
3 = DEF	**6 = MNO**	**9 = WXY**

(Answers for this section begin on page 309.)

Example:

Sweets

- 38343
- 22639   *candy*
- 46639

The answers are:
- fudge
- candy
- honey

Placement

- 34778 _____
- 84473 _____
- 34384 _____

Mammals

- 66673 _moose_____
- 46773 _horse_____
- 84437 _____

Sport Areas

- 87225 _____
- 34353 _____
- 26878 _____

Symphony

- 84652 _____
- 23556 _____
- 35883 _____

Bathroom

- 86935 _____

- 22746 _____

- 27874 _____

Fire

- 77275 _____

- 35263 _____

- 36237 _____

Close to the Ground

- 76253 _____

- 96767 _____

- 43256 _____

Clothes

- 74478 _____

- 72687 _____

- 76257 _____

Cuts

- 79673 _____

- 56433 _____

- 25233 _____

Sizes

- 44268 _____

- 76255 _____

- 52743 _____

Computer Peripherals

- 66873 _____

- 66336 _____

- 22253 _____

Yard

- 87337 _____

- 47277 _____

- 74782 _____

Measures

- 63837 _____
- 54837 _____
- 68623 _____

On the Table

- 77666 _____
- 56433 _____
- 75283 _____

Humor

- 38669 _____
- 26642 _____
- 52844 _____

Landscape

- 74343 _____
- 44559 _____
- 66863 _____

Legal Tender

- 66639 _____

- 26467 _____

- 23687 _____

See You in Court

- 58767 _____

- 58343 _____

- 25375 _____

Dinner

- 72782 _____

- 72523 _____

- 37465 _____

Body Joints

- 35269 _____

- 26553 _____

- 97478 _____

Six-Digit Numbers

Decode the digits to come up with six-letter words for each category. You are given the digits that are coded as on most telephones:

1	4 = GHI	7 = PRS
2 = ABC	5 = JKL	8 = TUV
3 = DEF	6 = MNO	9 = WXY

(Answers for this section begin on page 310.)

Example:

Toolbox

- 973624
- 426637
- 754377

The answers are:

- wrench
- hammer
- pliers

Talk

- 467747 _____
- 786677 _____
- 828853 _____

Colors

- 935569 _____
- 672643 _____
- 787753 _____

Elements

- 699436 _____
- 435486 _____
- 227266 _____

Taken

- 747633 _____
- 786536 _____
- 794733 _____

Composition

- 763879 _____

- 749637 _____

- 837737 _____

Space

- 425299 _____

- 752638 _____

- 728876 _____

Teeth

- 228489 _____

- 272237 _____

- 336825 _____

School

- 472337 _____

- 787457 _____

- 537766 _____

Films

- 727336 _____
- 668437 _____
- 246362 _____

Vision

- 738462 _____
- 267632 _____
- 393543 _____

Family

- 747837 _____
- 328437 _____
- 668437 _____

Ha Ha Ha

- 444453 _____
- 483329 _____
- 222553 _____

Thief

- 688529 _____

- 762237 _____

- 226348 _____

Speed

- 787433 _____

- 756959 _____

- 327837 _____

Time

- 732663 _____

- 646883 _____

- 332233 _____

Sports

- 762237 _____

- 836647 _____

- 462539 _____

Temperature

- 266537 _____

- 927637 _____

- 468837 _____

In the Office

- 267437 _____

- 736245 _____

- 746637 _____

Fruits

- 226262 _____

- 472737 _____

- 672643 _____

Dogs

- 232453 _____

- 265543 _____

- 766353 _____

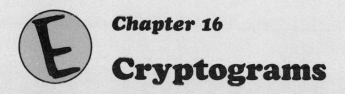

Chapter 16

Cryptograms

S hortly after humans started writing, they started using secret codes. Julius Caesar devised a simple code where he moved each letter three places up in the alphabet, so *A* became *D, B* became *E,* etc. Evidently this was effective for Caesar, but the codes used in this chapter are more advanced. For these puzzles, each letter of the alphabet is replaced by another letter, but the code changes from puzzle to puzzle. Your challenge is to decipher the coded text.

Cryptoquotes

In the following puzzles, each letter of the alphabet (A–Z) has been substituted with another letter. Your challenge is to break the code for each puzzle and decipher the quote and author. (Answers for this section begin on page 310.)

Example:

DCNHN BHN DCPTN ICP SPPU BD DCLYET DCN IBA DCNA BHN, BYK BTU ICA . . . L KHN-

BQ PV DCLYET DCBD YNONH INHN, BYK BTU ICA YPD?

—*HPXNHD UNYYNKA*

The answer is:

There are those who look at things the way they are, and ask why . . . I dream of things that never

were, and ask why not?

—*Robert Kennedy*

Cryptoquote Challenge 1

NJP IYKTVPU MW DKN NJRN NJPYP RYP IYKTVPUW. NJP IYKTVPU MW

PHIPGNMDB KNJPYXMWP RDE NJMDAMDB NJRN JRQMDB IYKTVPUW MW R

IYKTVPU.

—*NJPKEKYP YOTMD*

Cryptoquote Challenge 2

YGYCS IBQMT QV XH XCEQVE. EBY RCKUMYW QV BKO EK CYWXQH XH

XCEQVE KHIY BY FCKOV AR.

—*RXUMK RQIXVVK*

Cryptoquote Challenge 3

BODKOJRR QAYQUR XISDASJR OXRV; UDM PQI'C RCJQA RJPDIZ NQRJ QIZ

VJJB UDMO LDDC DI LXORC NQRJ.

—*LOJZJOXPV YXAPDF*

Cryptoquote Challenge 4

WVX'UB HBJBU SI KVVN SI BJBUWVHB ABRRI WVX ZEBH WVX ZOH, SHN

WVX'UB HBJBU SI CSN SI AEBW ISW ZEBH WVX RVIB.

—RVX EVRAM

Cryptoquote Challenge 5

VCECO ABZXR RLWR W FDWMM SOBZQ BT RLBZSLRTZM GBDDJRRCA QCBQMC

GWV GLWVSC RLC YBOMA: JVACCA JR'F RLC BVMP RLJVS RLWR CECO LWF!

—DWOSWOCR DCWAC

Cryptoquote Challenge 6

VADUDSXX AD PCZUX TZSJMSX TCDHAUSDTS. VADUDSXX AD MWADVADF

TZSJMSX LZCHCKDUDSXX. VADUDSXX AD FAQADF TZSJMSX ICQS.

—IJC MOK

Cryptoquote Challenge 7

SZASNM BJXJXVJB, IULJBM XSN LSUJ NID. VDU ULIMJ ALI LSUJ NID OIQ'U

AGQ DQZJMM NID LSUJ ULJX. SQO ULJQ NID OJMUBIN NIDBMJZH.

—*BGPLSBO X. QGFIQ*

Cryptoquote Challenge 8

J VNJTG VNUV BPWBRP QUTV BPUDP MW XYDN VNUV WTP WK VNPMP AUFM

ZWSPCTXPTVM NUA LPVVPC ZPV WYV WK VNP QUF UTA RPV VNPX NUSP JV.

—*AQJZNV A. PJMPTNWQPC*

Cryptoquote Challenge 9

GDO WUYNKOIH GDTG OFCHG CV GDO MYUKE GYETQ RTVVYG NO HYKXOE

NQ GDO KOXOK YS GDCVPCVB GDTG RUOTGOE GDOI.

—*TKNOUG OCVHGOCV*

Cryptoquote Challenge 10

BVKVKOVB UZFFGEVTT CAVTE'M CVFVEC YFAE RUA DAY ZBV AB RUZM DAY

UZLV; GM CVFVECT TAXVXD AE RUZM DAY MUGEI.

—CZXV QZBEVJGV

Cryptoquote Challenge 11

PNIQ LYQ Y HIGLVK KIIEL UBLP PNGII PNJKXL PV TI PGBOQ NYHHQ JK PNJL

MVGOE: LVZIVKI PV OVFI, LVZIPNJKX PV EV, YKE LVZIPNJKX PV NVHI CVG.

—PVZ TVEIPP

Cryptoquote Challenge 12

J UA HBFHUBFC YX CJF, QEY YSFBF JW TX GUEWF LXB KSJGS J UA

HBFHUBFC YX VJPP.

—AUSUYAU OUTCSJ

Cryptoquote Challenge 13

INOG TGP KZYJ VGXZHOG KMGA MZLG OETGKMNPR KE OZA; CEEYO,

VGXZHOG KMGA MZLG KE OZA OETGKMNPR.

—*SYZKE*

Cryptoquote Challenge 14

KNP YPRK FBV KZ UNPPT VZMTRPES QR KZ KTV KZ UNPPT RZHPZOP

PERP MJ.

—*HBTI KFBQO*

Cryptoquote Challenge 15

BRCT GZN RQSC MZTHPICTMC, GZN MQT RQSC Q JZE ZH HNT. QTI BRCT

GZN RQSC HNT, GZN MQT IZ QOQFPTV ERPTVK.

—*YZC TQOQER*

Cryptoquote Challenge 16

TK BOS TW XQWCSY BK BOS CGTOR QOZ POZSYWCQOZW BOS CGTOR JSFF,

BOS GQW QC CGS WQXS CTXS, TOWTRGC TOCB QOZ POZSYWCQOZTOR BK

XQOL CGTORW.

—*ITOASOC IQO RBRG*

Cryptoquote Challenge 17

N IWF SBM DWCT YBST VDTKT N NSMTSGTG MB YB, JLM N MDNSE N DWCT

TSGTG LX VDTKT N NSMTSGTG MB JT.

—*GBLYRWH WGWIH*

Cryptoquote Challenge 18

NUQ ZWL XKHZUPRM FUMR WCUQB W ARMHUL KL WL EUQM UT AVWN

BEWL KL W NRWM UT ZULPRMHWBKUL.

—*AVWBU*

Cryptoquote Challenge 19

G BVNR QTHWF DBR PRYD IVO DT SGNR VFNGXR DT OTHM XBGAFMRW GY

DT QGWF THD IBVD DBRO IVWD VWF DBRW VFNGYR DBRC DT FT GD.

—*BVMMO Y DMHCVW*

Cryptoquote Challenge 20

UGL KYYA FLYFSL XSLLF TDZG NLUULO CU IPKGU UGCI UGL NCA FLYFSL.

YQ ZYDOXL, UGL NCA FLYFSL LIRYV UGL MCEPIK GYDOX TDZG TYOL.

—*MYYAV CSSLI*

Cryptoquote Challenge 21

DFEWQ DLR ZRWG DRCD FI TFNRZ XC VFD HWTWHXDQ DF BWOR NWZ

YPD DLR HWTWHXDQ DF TZRMRVD XD.

—*WVVR F'LWZR BHHFZBXHO*

Cryptoquote Challenge 22

KWMYSMYZ MU KWA AYAEX NC BFAJKMOMKX. MK'U UAGC-BNYUBMNIU,

JYR JYXKWMYZ UAGC-BNYUBMNIU MU GNIUX. XNI BJY'K KFX KN RN KWMYZU.

XNI UMETGX EIUK RN KWMYZU.

—FJX HFJRHIFX

Cryptoquote Challenge 23

MGN RNMHNKQQ WQ W FWAP.MF EWF CK FM QJPZAKN ALWF MGN

RNMHNKQQ PF KXGEWAPMF. ALK LGSWF SPFX PQ MGN ZGFXWSKFAWI

NKQMGNEK.

—VMLF Z. UKFFKXT

Cryptoquote Challenge 24

UYN MPVVNHNDEN ANUFNND UYN HPQYU FIHM KDM UYN KTSILU HPQYU

FIHM PL UYN MPVVNHNDEN ANUFNND TPQYUDPDQ KDM K TPQYUDPDQ AOQ.

—SKHW UFKPD

Cryptoquote Challenge 25

S UHXXHV XYMOSTF OASO BFHBEF XSTF CAFV OLZYVP OH JFMYPV

MHXFOAYVP UHXBEFOFZ QHHEBLHHQ YM OH RVJFLFMOYXSOF OAF

YVPFVRYOZ HQ UHXBEFOF QHHEM.

—*JHRPESM SJSXM*

Cryptoquote Challenge 26

NI BKI ACBSIJ YG ETK FCETDCFA; NI YIZERI NCBF NI FCPLH. NCIL FCI RPLJ

PA STKI, XEG QEVVENA VPHI B ACBJEN FCBF LIUIK VIBUIA.

—*YTJJCB*

Cryptoquote Challenge 27

ICH VDDVIHKTIH LP ICH PQIQKH NVDD FLI EH ICH JHKULF NCL RTFFLI

KHTX. VI NVDD EH ICH JHKULF NCL XLHU FLI OFLN CLN IL DHTKF.

—*TDGVF ILPPDHK*

Cryptoquote Challenge 28

DJT KCT ZTMG FJ QCSSG OQJT BQJG NZ TZB CXXADJ BQCB BQJ ZFVJKB ZE

MPEJ PX QCSSPTJXX.

—HJZUHJ ZUOJMM

Cryptoquote Challenge 29

GCRRQGG FG KMJ JXQ SQO JM XDEEFKQGG. XDEEFKQGG FG JXQ SQO JM

GCRRQGG. FB OMC IMYQ ZXDJ OMC DTQ WMFKU, OMC ZFII VQ GCRRQGGBCI.

—XQTNDK RDFK

Cryptoquote Challenge 30

CAXVLFLN RQH CXTV VQ UQ, UQ DV TQC. VALNL XNL QTPR ZQ GXTR

VQGQNNQCZ.

—GDIAXLP PXTUQT

Cryptolists

Each letter of the alphabet (A–Z) has been substituted with another letter in the coded text. Your challenge is to break the code for each puzzle and decipher the list. (Answers for this section begin on page 312.)

Example:

C Vegetables

KLJJLDB	KBYBVG	KNVH
KLVVNU	KIQKAEBL	KXKXSJBV
KLXYQRYNPBV		

The answers are:

cabbage	celery	corn
carrot	chickpea	cucumber
cauliflower		

U.S. Holidays	Shakespeare
ASCBAL	WXFMUV QN WGP IGKPZ
KRLECBFSC	X FMLIRFFPK UMVGW'I LKPXF
BRSYQCMEHEYM	KQFPQ XUL BRTMPW
YAO UASL'C VSU	FROG XLQ XYQRW UQWGMUV
XZTLBR ZX GTNU	GXFTPW
FAFZLESN VSU	XTT'I ZPTT WGXW PULI ZPTT
NSJZL VSU	FXOYPWG

Insects	Beatles Songs
MDLZAX	"K SKLA AKF'E TDISU"
UJQGNKF	"HJMG OG AJ"
NKXXALRUG	"CKCGLYKZQ NLDUGL"
UDTKEX	"SGF BVAG"
SDEVKBXD	"D KO USG NKHLVE"
TLBTWAX	"HGU DU YG"
FLJEEMDHHAL	"D NKTU UJ SJHA FJVL SKTA"

Office Supplies	Classic Literature
JPGHQIM	OMB YXZBGOJPBL WK OWS LYEIBP
JPGM	XWG AJUFWOB
JOJPY	XP. VBNITT YGX SP. MIXB
JOJPYHIQJM	OMB LHYPTBO TBOOBP
MHQMMXYM	Y OYTB WK OEW HUOUBL
JYAIPY	OMB OUSB SYHMUGB
MZOJIPY	OPBYLJPB ULTYGX

Gems	**Automobile**
ZKSVMQZ	NUDWA
TVTLSBZ	TUGHACUWRH
RSLQTW	ANWWDUGY TCWWR
MJSB	YRZBW SZJOFDNJWGN
LDOX	DFHUZ
CSJJUKLT	ZHZJWNWD
WDLYDMKCT	AOWWHZJWNWD

U.S. National Parks	Movies
STLRJ ZLRCAR	*LBOQBOS OXVH*
CAOKUWPK	*ZFKWX IAVBSRCT*
CKIIABOPARK	*VXO BO ZAIWN*
SILZWKT HLC	*EPXXC RHVX IAIZIVI*
STLRJ PKPAR	*GAIOXC HL CRX IGXE*
TAZXC UAERPLWR	*I ZXIKCBLKA VBOQ*
HTCZK ZLRCAR	*IVXFBWIO ZXIKCT*

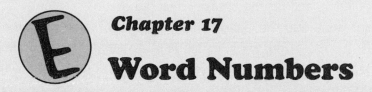

Chapter 17

Word Numbers

Are you a numbers person or a word person? For this chapter, it helps to be both. The challenges here explore interesting links between letters and numbers. Many of the puzzles in this chapter have ancient origins, which is not surprising since historians tell us that written numbers have been around for at least as long as letters.

Roman Numeral Chronograms

Chronograms are words with hidden numbers. These chronograms contain an extra challenge; Roman numerals. For the chronogram puzzles in this section, first take the number given in each phrase and convert it into Roman numeral letters. Next, find a word that contains that set of letters and fits the phrase's description.

Roman numerals are represented in the customary way, as combinations of these seven letters: I=1, V=5, X=10, L=50, C=100, D=500, M=1000. If a smaller letter follows a larger letter, the numbers are added. If a smaller letter precedes a larger letter, the numbers are subtracted. In other words; VI=6, IV=4.(Answers for this section begin on page 313.)

Example:
4 homes for bees

The answer is *hive* because it contains the letters *IV,* the Roman numeral for *4.*

Chronogram Challenge 1

- 16 Tennessee cities

_____

- 101 types of apple juice

_____

- 51 rooms with books

_____

Chronogram Challenge 2

- 91 energized

_____

- 11 leaving the building

_____

- 1,101 apples, not the computer

_____

Chronogram Challenge 3

- 1,051 designed for efficiency   _____

- 2,000 season   _____

- 400 amusing accounts   _____

Chronogram Challenge 4

- 1,500 chewy candies covered with sugar   _____

- 1,009 combinations   _____

- 54 Mediterranean fruits   _____

Chronogram Challenge 5

- 650 palm beatings   _____

- 40 wheel shafts   _____

- 2,001 new residents   _____

Chronogram Challenge 6

- 1,001 rodents   _____

- 90 outstanding   _____

- 502 distances from the center   _____

Chronogram Challenge 7

- 55 second-place Olympic medals _____

- 41 resembling a crafty mammal _____

- 6 small settlements _____

Chronogram Challenge 8

- 600 built from sand at the beach _____

- 59 cure-all concoctions _____

- 2 states _____

Chronogram Challenge 9

- 9 presidents _____

- 1,050 Shakespeare Danish princes _____

- 56 rock 'n' roll kings _____

Chronogram Challenge 10

- 551 newspaper titles _____

- 1,100 master of ceremonies _____

- 504 jumping from airplanes _____

Number Name Chronograms

Fill in the blanks with words that contain the names of the numbers given in the title. (Answers for this section begin on page 313.)

Example:

Number Name Chronogram: 1-2-10

She wrote the letter on _____ that featured abstract _____ that her son did in his _____ class.

The answer is:

She wrote the letter on STATI**ONE**RY that featured abstract AR**TWO**RK that her son did in his KINDERGAR**TEN** class.

Number Name Chronogram: 2-10-8

The fancy _____ of the boxer is what made him a _____ against the _____ champion.

Number Name Chronogram: 1-10-1

The epitaph " _____ but not _____" was etched in _____.

Number Name Chronogram: 8-10-1

The ship carried _____ that he _____ to sell in Canada for a

lot of _____.

Number Name Chronogram: 2-10-2

Clint _____ played police _____ Speer in the movie *City*

Heat which played on the ABC television _____ last night.

Number Name Chronogram: 1-1-1

The _____ felt very _____ in solitary confinement after

hearing that his trial was _____ again.

Number Name Chronogram: 10-10-8

She held a _____ for her invention of a radio _____ that

required a _____ of only five feet.

Number Name Chronogram: 10-9-10

As we _____ to the lecture, the professor classified the dog as

a _____ and the _____ as a feline.

Number Name Chronogram: 8-1-10

The _____ of the load made the porter's _____ ache and

required his full _____ to keep it balanced.

Number Name Chronogram: 10-1-1

She _____ told him to please _____ me _____

rather than later.

Number Name Chronogram: 1-8-10

_____ of his _____ of hand tricks worked when he was

wearing _____ that covered his fingers.

Cryptarithms

A cryptarithm is a puzzle where numbers are substituted for letters to correctly complete an arithmetic equation. These types of puzzles originated thousands of years ago in China. Your challenge is to determine the numbers that can correctly be substituted for the letters. The same number must be substituted for the same letter throughout the equation. Some people find trial and error the best method to hone in on a solution. (Answers for this section begin on page 313.)

Example:

```
      T    W    O
  +   T    W    O
  ─────────────────
  F    O    U    R
```

(Hint: *F* must be "1" since that is the only number that can be carried from the previous column.)

There are seven possible solutions:

938+938=1,876	836+836=1,672	846+846=1,692	867+867=1,734
928+928=1,856	765+765=1,530	734+734=1,468	

Cryptarithm Challenge 1

```
                I
  +    Y    O    U
  ─────────────────
       A    L    L
```

There are twenty possible solutions.

Cryptarithm Challenge 2

```
       D    A    D
  +    M    O    M
  ─────────────────
  B    A    B    Y
```

There are six possible solutions.

Cryptarithm Challenge 3

```
    O   N   E
+   O   N   E
─────────────
    T   W   O
```

There are sixteen possible solutions.

Cryptarithm Challenge 4

```
        W   A   L   L
+       R   O   O   F
─────────────────────
    H   O   U   S   E
```

There are sixteen possible solutions.

Cryptarithm Challenge 5

```
    H   E   E   L
+   T   O   E   S
─────────────────
    S   H   O   E
```

There are seven possible solutions.

Cryptarithm Challenge 6

```
        R   O   C   K
+       R   O   L   L
─────────────────────
    M   U   S   I   C
```

There are eighteen possible solutions.

Cryptarithm Challenge 7

```
    B   R   I   D   E
+   G   R   O   O   M
─────────────────────
W   E   D   D   E   D
```

There are two possible solutions.

Cryptarithm Challenge 8

```
        P   E   A   R
+   G   R   A   P   E
─────────────────────
    F   R   U   I   T
```

There are fifteen possible solutions.

Cryptarithm Challenge 9

```
    V   E   R   B
+   N   O   U   N
─────────────────
W   O   R   D   S
```

There are ten possible solutions.

Cryptarithm Challenge 10

```
    W   O   R   D   S
+   G   A   M   E   S
─────────────────────
    A   M   U   S   E
```

There are fourteen possible solutions.

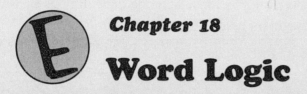

Chapter 18

Word Logic

A popular theory suggests that your brain has two sides. The right side is intuitive and emotional, while the left side is logical and rational. The beauty of word games is that they can potentially exercise both sides of your brain. The logic puzzles in this chapter will focus on the left side of your brain.

Dr. Rational

Dr. Rational has very definite preferences—however, his preferences are based on the letters in the underlying words, not the actual things the words describe. For each puzzle you are given three examples that illustrate one of the rules for Dr. Rational's preferences. Your challenge is to determine the pattern and decide which one of two things Dr. Rational prefers. (Answers for this section begin on page 315.)

Example:

- Dr. Rational likes green but not blue.

- Dr. Rational likes wheels but not tires.

- Dr. Rational likes freezers but not refrigerators.

Does Dr. Rational like RIVERS or CREEKS?

Answer:
Dr. Rational likes creeks, because *creeks* has a double vowel.

Dr. Rational Challenge 1

- Dr. Rational likes to draw but not to color.
- Dr. Rational likes shoes but not socks.
- Dr. Rational likes whales but not dolphins.

Does Dr. Rational like SEVEN or EIGHT?

Dr. Rational Challenge 2

- Dr. Rational likes Spot but not Rover.
- Dr. Rational likes that but not this.
- Dr. Rational likes height but not size.

Does Dr. Rational like GINGER or BRIDGET?

Dr. Rational Challenge 3

- Dr. Rational likes nuts but not popcorn.
- Dr. Rational likes Bob but not Joe.
- Dr. Rational likes rats but not mice.

Does Dr. Rational like GOOD or EVIL?

Dr. Rational Challenge 4

- Dr. Rational likes gowns but not dresses.
- Dr. Rational likes knowledge but not trivia.
- Dr. Rational likes pawns but not kings.

Does Dr. Rational like SAWS or HAMMERS?

Dr. Rational Challenge 5

- Dr. Rational likes streets but not avenues.
- Dr. Rational likes hips but not waists.
- Dr. Rational likes deer but not moose.

Does Dr. Rational like MIDNIGHT or NOON?

Dr. Rational Challenge 6

- Dr. Rational likes Alaska but not Hawaii.
- Dr. Rational likes Panama but not Belize.
- Dr. Rational likes alfalfa but not hay.

Does Dr. Rational like ANAGRAMS or CRYPTOGRAMS?

Dr. Rational Challenge 7

- Dr. Rational likes archery but not hunting.
- Dr. Rational likes spheres but not globes.
- Dr. Rational likes bleachers but not stadiums.

Does Dr. Rational like PEACHES or CHERRIES?

Dr. Rational Challenge 8

- Dr. Rational likes states but not cities.
- Dr. Rational likes graphing but not drawing.
- Dr. Rational likes exercise but not aerobics.

Does Dr. Rational like INDIANA or OHIO?

Dr. Rational Challenge 9

- Dr. Rational likes slate but not writing.
- Dr. Rational likes to steal but not to cheat.
- Dr. Rational likes teals but not blues.

Does Dr. Rational like TALES or STORIES?

Dr. Rational Challenge 10

- Dr. Rational likes crypts but not vaults.
- Dr. Rational likes rhythm but not beat.
- Dr. Rational likes myths but not stories.

Does Dr. Rational like HYMNS or SONGS?

Dr. Rational Challenge 11

- Dr. Rational likes refrigerators but not freezers.
- Dr. Rational likes teepees but not tents.
- Dr. Rational likes bassists but not violinists.

Does Dr. Rational like NOVELS or COOK-BOOKS?

Dr. Rational Challenge 12

- Dr. Rational likes equations but not mathematics.
- Dr. Rational likes sequoias but not evergreens.
- Dr. Rational likes dialogue but not conversation.

Does Dr. Rational like AUDIOTAPE or VIDEO-TAPE?

Dr. Rational Challenge 13

- Dr. Rational likes noon but not lunch.
- Dr. Rational likes in but not out.
- Dr. Rational likes the zoo but not cages.

Does Dr. Rational like ANN or SUE?

Dr. Rational Challenge 14

- Dr. Rational likes janitors but not cleaners.
- Dr. Rational likes decaf but not coffee.
- Dr. Rational likes novices but not beginners.

Does Dr. Rational like JADEITE or AUGITE?

Dr. Rational Challenge 15

- Dr. Rational likes one but not two.
- Dr. Rational likes good but not great.
- Dr. Rational likes here but not there.

Does Dr. Rational like PRETTY or CUTE?

Letter States

Determine the letters that are common to all three given words. Then rearrange these letters to make the name of a U.S. state. (Answers for this section begin on page 315.)

Example:

- comedian
- dairymen
- examiner

All three words contain the letters *M, E, I, A, N.*
The answer is *Maine.*

Letter States Challenge 1

- choirboy
- chocoholics
- autobiographers

Letter States Challenge 2

- groomsmen
- wrongdoer
- ergonomist

Letter States Challenge 3

- blacksnakes
- rattlesnakes
- knapsacks

Letter States Challenge 4

- millionaires
- multidimensional
- illusionist

Letter States Challenge 5

- informative
- government
- improvement

Letter States Challenge 6

- holiday
- fashioned
- humanoids

Letter States Challenge 7

- advanced
- navigated
- heavenward

Letter States Challenge 8

- imagination
- tantamount
- animation

Letter States Challenge 9

- baklavas
- lackadaisical
- balkanizations

Letter States Challenge 10

- verbalization
- organizable
- vaporization

Letter States Challenge 11

- postdoctoral
- bachelorhood
- discoloration

Letter States Challenge 12

- exaltations
- hatboxes
- transfixed

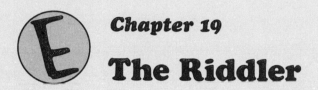

Chapter 19

The Riddler

The riddle is the oldest type of word game and is found in nearly every culture throughout history. Riddles were important in religion and philosophy as a means for sages to express their wisdom. But riddles are also just plain fun, as you will find out in this chapter. One friendly piece of advice: Don't spoil the fun by looking at the answer section too fast!

Riddles

Solve these riddle challenges. They come from a variety of places and eras. (Answers for this section begin on page 315.)

Riddle of the Sphinx

What walks on four legs in the morning, two legs at noon, and three in the evening?

> —*In the Greek legend, this riddle was solved by Oedipus who became king of Thebes as a reward.*

Ends in -GRY

Think of words ending in *-gry*. Angry and hungry are two of them. There are only three words in the English language. What is the third word? The word is something that everyone uses every day. If you have listened carefully, I have already told you what it is.

Children

I have a bunch of children.
When the sun comes out, they hide,
When the sun hides, they come out.

> —*From the Island of Mauritius*

Sings

Round as a hoop, deep as a pail;
Never sings out till it's caught by the tail.

> —*From Newfoundland*

Lawyer, Soldier, Sailor

A Russian had three sons. The first, named Rab, became a lawyer. The second, Ymra, became a soldier. The third became a sailor; what was his name?

> —*By Lewis Carroll, in a June 1892 diary entry*

Fishermen

A riddle posed to Homer by some fishermen:

What we caught we left behind, but what we failed to catch we brought with us.

(Some say that Homer died of frustration at being unable to solve this riddle.)

Begin and End

The beginning of eternity,
The end of time and space,
The beginning of every end,
And the end of every place.

Long and Short

What of all things in the world is the longest and the shortest, swiftest and the slowest, the most divisible and the most extended, the most neglected and the most regretted, without which nothing can be done. Which devours all that is little and enlivens all that is great.

—By Voltaire (1694–1778)

Flying

I am the black child of a white father;
A wingless bird, flying even to the clouds of heaven.
I give birth to tears of mourning in pupils that meet me,
and at once on my birth I am dissolved into air.

—From ancient Greece

Touch Me

If you break me
I do not stop working,
If you touch me
I may be snared,
If you lose me
Nothing will matter.

Three Letters

I know a word of letters three.
Add two, and fewer there will be.

Waves Over Me

Sea suckled me, waves sounded over me,
rollers covered me as I rested on my bed.
I have no feet and often open my mouth
to the flood. Now some man will
consume me, who cares nothing for my clothing.
With the point of his knife he will rip the skin
away from my side, and straight away eat me
uncooked as I am.

*—From the Exeter
Book (circa A.D. 975)*

Related

Brothers and sisters have I none, but that man's father is my father's son.

Behead

As a whole, I am both safe and secure.

Behead me, and I become a place of meeting.

Behead me again, and I am the partner of ready.

Restore me, and I become the domain of beasts.

Devoured

My life can be measured in hours,
I serve by being devoured.
Thin, I am quick
Fat, I am slow
Wind is my foe.

Enigmas

An enigma is a riddle written in verse. Here is a collection of enigmas for you to solve. (Answers for this section begin on page 316.)

The Rich Require

What does man love more than life
Fear more than death or mortal strife
What the poor have, the rich require,
and what contented men desire,
What the miser spends and the spendthrift saves
And all men carry to their graves?

Two and Two

I am just two and two, I am warm, I am cold,
And the parent of numbers that cannot be told:
I am lawful, unlawful—a duty, a fault,
I am often sold dear, good for nothing when bought,
An extraordinary boon, and a matter of course,
And yielded with pleasure when taken by force.

—By William Cowper, July 1780

A Breed Unfit

Unlike my mother, in semblance different from my father,
of mingled race, a breed unfit for progeny,
of others am I born, and none is born of me.

—By Symphosius in the fourth century A.D.

Breathe

I do not straightway die while breath departs;
for repeatedly it returns, though often too departs again:
and now my store of vital breath is great, now none.

—By Symphosius in the fourth century A.D.

Sixty

Six eyes are mine; as many ears have I;
Fingers and toes twice thirty do I bear.
Of these, when forty from my flesh are torn,
Lo, then but twenty will remain to me.

—By Aldhelm, a seventh-century English poet

Never and Always

I never was, am always to be,
No one ever saw me, nor ever will
And yet I am the confidence of all
To live and breathe on this terrestrial ball.

Strange Indeed

My sides are firmly laced about,
Yet nothing is within;
You'll think my head is strange indeed,
Being nothing else but skin.

—From the Guess Book, by William Davidson (1781–1858)

Airy Creatures

We are little airy Creatures,
All of diff'rent Voice and Features,
One of us in Glass is set,
One of us you'll find in Jet,
T'other you may see in Tin,
And the fourth a Box within,
If the fifth you shou'd pursue,
It can never fly from you.

—By Jonathan Swift (1667–1745)

Eat

Ever eating, never cloying,
All-devouring, all-destroying,
Never finding full repast,
Till I eat the world at last.

—By Jonathan Swift (1667–1745)

Clamorous

I'm named after nothing,
Though I'm awfully clamorous,
And when I'm not working,
Your house is less glamorous.

A Yellow Fork

I am, in truth, a yellow fork
From tables in the sky
By inadvertent fingers dropped
The awful cutlery.
Of mansions never quite disclosed
And never quite concealed
The apparatus of the dark
To ignorance revealed.

—By Emily Dickinson (1830–1886)

Play

Four people sat down at a table to play;
They play'd all that night, and some part of the next day:
This one thing observ'd, that when they were seated,
Nobody played with them, and nobody betted:
Yet when they got up, each was winner a guinea;
Who tells me this riddle, I'm sure is no ninny.

—Sir Isaac Newton, 1773

Suspended in Air

I'm not in earth, nor the sun, nor the moon;
You may search all the sky—I'm not there.
In the morning and evening—though not in the noon—
You may plainly perceive me, for like a balloon,
I am midway suspended in air.
Though disease may possess me, and sickness and pain,
I am never in sorrow nor gloom;
Though in wit and wisdom I equally reign,
I'm the heart of all sin, and have long lived in vain,
Yet I ne'er shall be found in the tomb.

—Lord Byron (1788–1824)

Under the Sea

Oft I must strive with wind and wave,
Battle them both when under the sea
I feel out the bottom, a foreign land.
In lying still I am strong in the strife;
If I fail in that they are stronger than I,
And wrenching me loose, soon put me to rout.
They wish to capture what I must keep.
I can master them both if my grip holds out,
If the rocks bring succor and lend support,
Strength in the struggle. Ask me my name!

—From the Exeter Book (circa A.D. 975)

Letter Rebuses

A rebus is a puzzle made up of pictures and letters, sort of a visual riddle. The puzzles presented here use letters. For example, IOU translates to "I owe you." That one was really easy; now try your hand at these harder rebus challenges. (Answers for this section begin on page 316.)

Up and Down

control
everything

_____

man
board

_____

wear
long

_____

Neighbors

death life

_____

he he himself

_____

I'M you

_____

Within

scotheop

_____

poFISHnd

_____

tiastitchme

_____

Backwords

ecnalg

_____

nar eh he ran

_____

gnikool
1999
2000
2001

_____

Double

dice dice

_____

aallll

_____

des des

_____

Broken

hou se

_____

gegs

_____

cof fee

_____

Sports

issues issues issues issues issues
issues issues issues issues issues

_____

leftoutfield

_____

dribble dribble

_____

Letters Only

HIJKLMNO

_____

M, E

_____

ABCDEFGHIJKMNOPQRSTUVWXYZ

_____

Phraseology

paid
I'm
worked

_____

YYURYYUBICURYY4ME

_____

ALL world

_____

Stuck Key

_____

The &EEEE

_____

XQQQ

_____

EEEEEEEEEEC

_____

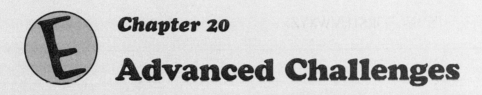

Chapter 20

Advanced Challenges

I t is time to explore the outer boundaries of word puzzles. Of course, words seem to have no limits. For example, when Mary Poppins sang the song "Supercalifragilistic-expialidocious" she helped create one of the longest words in the English language, which is now found in some dictionaries. This chapter revisits some of the earlier puzzle types and pushes them to their limits.

Anagram Titles

These puzzles are longer versions of the anagrams found in Chapter 2. Rearrange the letters in the given words to form titles. (Answers for this section begin on page 316.)

Hemingway Books

1. *MANHATTAN HEEDS DOLE*

_____

2. *A THORNLESS ISSUE*

_____

3. *REFORMAT SEAWALL*

_____

Rodgers and Hammerstein

1. *FAT SATIRE*

_____

2. *SEDUCTION OF HUMS*

_____

3. *FUCHSIA TOPIC*

_____

1980s Television Shows

1. *STOKE HARDHEAD FUZZ*

   _____

2. *A BEVEL TOOTH*

   _____

3. *HEALTHIER SOUL PETITIONER*

   _____

Elvis Presley Songs

1. "TENURED SNORTER"

   _____

2. "DENVER OMELET"

   _____

3. "NEGOTIATES UNHOLY ROMEO"

   _____

Harrison Ford Movies

1. *RAILROADERS THEFTS OK*

   _____

2. *SLENDER RANGER TAPDANCE*

   _____

3. *CARRIE NO FOE*

   _____

Multiple Transadditions

These puzzles are five-step versions of the transadditions in Chapter 5. Start by solving the first clue to get a four-letter word. Then solve each of the following clues by adding the appropriate letter to the word from the previous step and rearranging the letters. If you get stuck, you may want to try working backwards. (Answers for this section begin on page 316.)

Example:

1. It is seen in a forest.

2. Add an *A* to get someone who must be hungry.

3. Add an *S* to get an ad arousing curiosity.

4. Add a *W* for something to keep you warm.

5. Add an *A* to fill the ocean.

The answers are:

1. tree

2. eater

3. teaser

4. sweater

5. seawater

Multiple Transaddition Challenge 1

1. They have nine lives. _____

2. Add an *O* and get tortilla treats. _____

3. Add an *R* and get people on stage. _____

4. Add a *C* and you can set your drink on it. _____

5. Add an *N* and you get a person from your past. _____

Multiple Transaddition Challenge 2

1. It is a thorny flower. _____

2. Add an *H* and get a hoofed animal. _____

3. Add a *C* and get routine tasks. _____

4. Add an *A* and get household pests. _____

5. Add a *P* and get illegal hunters. _____

Multiple Transaddition Challenge 3

1. Would you _____ to join me? _____

2. Add a *T* and get a barely perceivable amount. _____

3. Add an *N* and get a sweet liquid. _____

Multiple Transaddition Challenge 3—continued

4. Add an *I* and be sure. _____

5. Add an *L* and get a woodwind instrument. _____

Multiple Transaddition Challenge 4

1. Your money or your _____. _____

2. Add an *R* and get a firearm. _____

3. Add an *F* and get a straining device. _____

4. Add an *S* and get things of little importance. _____

5. Add a *B* and get hazelnuts. _____

Multiple Transaddition Challenge 5

1. The value of a penny. _____

2. Add an *S* to get a smell. _____

3. Add an *I* to get a small arthropod. _____

4. Add an *L* to get customers. _____

5. Add an *S* to get a pattern for lettering. _____

Six-Letter Word Ladders

These puzzles are six-letter versions of the word ladders found in Chapter 6. Link these six-letter words together with a ladder of words. Each step in the ladder must be a word, and must differ from the previous word by only one letter. There are many possible solutions, but try to use only the given number of steps. (Answers for this section begin on page 317.)

TICKET to TRAINS

T   I   C   K   E   T

_____ _____ _____ _____ _____ _____

_____ _____ _____ _____ _____ _____

_____ _____ _____ _____ _____ _____

_____ _____ _____ _____ _____ _____

_____ _____ _____ _____ _____ _____

_____ _____ _____ _____ _____ _____

_____ _____ _____ _____ _____ _____

_____ _____ _____ _____ _____ _____

_____ _____ _____ _____ _____ _____

_____ _____ _____ _____ _____ _____

T   R   A   I   N   S

FASTER to SLOWER

F   A   S   T   E   R

_____   _____   _____   _____   _____   _____

_____   _____   _____   _____   _____   _____

_____   _____   _____   _____   _____   _____

_____   _____   _____   _____   _____   _____

_____   _____   _____   _____   _____   _____

_____   _____   _____   _____   _____   _____

_____   _____   _____   _____   _____   _____

_____   _____   _____   _____   _____   _____

S   L   O   W   E   R

CROOKS to CRIMES

C   R   O   O   K   S

_____   _____   _____   _____   _____   _____

_____   _____   _____   _____   _____   _____

_____   _____   _____   _____   _____   _____

_____   _____   _____   _____   _____   _____

C   R   I   M   E   S

GOLFER to SPORTS

G	O	L	F	E	R
____	____	____	____	____	____
____	____	____	____	____	____
____	____	____	____	____	____
____	____	____	____	____	____
____	____	____	____	____	____
____	____	____	____	____	____
____	____	____	____	____	____
____	____	____	____	____	____
____	____	____	____	____	____
____	____	____	____	____	____
S	P	O	R	T	S

LISTEN to BUGLER

L   I   S   T   E   N

_____   _____   _____   _____   _____   _____

_____   _____   _____   _____   _____   _____

_____   _____   _____   _____   _____   _____

_____   _____   _____   _____   _____   _____

_____   _____   _____   _____   _____   _____

B   U   G   L   E   R

Four-Letter Ghosts

These are similar to the ghosts puzzles in Chapter 8, except here your task here is to find at least three words that contain a given sequence of *four* letters. (Answers for this section begin on page 317.)

Example:

Sequence: VALI

Answers could include: ca**vali**er, in**vali**d, and revi**vali**sm

Sequence: ESSO

1. _____

2. _____

3. _____

Sequence: ENCI

1. _____

2. _____

3. _____

Sequence: RASE

1. _____

2. _____

3. _____

Sequence: NDAR

1. _____

2. _____

3. _____

Sequence: EASU

1. _____

2. _____

3. _____

Sequence: EALI

1. _____

2. _____

3. _____

Quintuplets

These are similar to the triplets puzzles found in Chapter 10, except here you will be dealing with groups of five compound words. Determine the common word that can be combined with each of the five given words. (Answers for this section begin on page 317.)

Quintuplets Challenge 1

1. works   _____

2. wild   _____

3. man   _____

4. camp   _____

5. cross   _____

Quintuplets Challenge 3

1. fish   _____

2. light   _____

3. super   _____

4. ship   _____

5. gaze   _____

Quintuplets Challenge 2

1. bed   _____

2. plate   _____

3. cake   _____

4. red   _____

5. wire   _____

Quintuplets Challenge 4

1. night   _____

2. back   _____

3. pit   _____

4. out   _____

5. water   _____

Quintuplets Challenge 5

1. piece   _____

2. time   _____

3. corn   _____

4. worm   _____

5. oat   _____

Spaceless Cryptoquotes

These are advanced versions of the crytpoquote puzzles found in Chapter 16. For these puzzles all of the punctuation has been removed. Each letter of the alphabet (A–Z) has been substituted with another letter in the coded text. The space between words has also been substituted with a letter in the coded text. Your challenge is to break the code for each puzzle and decipher the quote and author. As a hint, all of the quotes are from U.S. presidents. (Answers for this section begin on page 318.)

Example:

FVSGOVGKXHGHVSGOKWGVQKGKXHGRHFEWGOVGRQAEGN

OJHGKXFKGYQAVKGOKWGKXHGNOJHGOVGRQAEGRHFEW

FTEFXFUGNOVYQNV

The answer is:
And in the end, it's not the years in your life that count. It's the life in your years.
          —*Abraham Lincoln*

Spaceless Cryptoquote Challenge 1

YZECKCJVNVEEYFRCLDVRCTFGJCRVYHDXFJCPFEVECDY

ECIFXCYZECKCSVAJVEEYFRCLDVRCTFGCPFEVCTFGJE

—*DKJJTCECZJGBKR*

Spaceless Cryptoquote Challenge 2

XJNOJQGGZNVXOYFYNTXVOFUOYROAZUNOJQINOHNN

TOXJNOUNSOSJZEJOZOJQINOGQVVNMOQXOJFYNOZT

OXJNOHFVFYOFUOYROUQYZAR

—*XJFYQVOPNUUNBVFT*

Spaceless Cryptoquote Challenge 3

YFHVKMFNEAQTNUCNTEKPFNYFFANUANOGFNXFFJFM

ONPVQQFTNHVANTEKNFPFZNDAEINGEINLVRAUCUHF

AONUONUMNOENYFNEANOGFNGURGFMONLEKAOVUA

—*ZUHGVZXNLNAUSEA*

Spaceless Cryptoquote Challenge 4

WZQLVLBYNLYNYJWWZYDPNVZNHDNVODNYDBZRPNZQ

PDYVNWFZTDYYLZRNLNOUSDNBZGDNVZNFDUQLKDNV

OUVNLVNHDUFYNUNSDFXNBQZYDNFDYDGHQURBDNVZ

NVODNTLFYV

—FZRUQPNFDUCUR

Spaceless Cryptoquote Challenge 5

SNBCPUHXBOPHIBPHBXDBHGGBXIPHBFYVTLGBDCBS

VJQPJABOVUDWVJPIIIGABCUDSBXIGBGVUXI

—TGDUTGBOVHIPJTXDJ

Appendix A

Answers

Chapter 1: Scramblers

Knocking at Your Door

"A pessimist sees the difficulty in every opportunity; an optimist sees the opportunity in every difficulty."

—*Sir Winston Churchill*

Hard Work

"Genius is one percent inspiration and ninety-nine percent perspiration."

—*Thomas Edison*

The Good Life

"Dance like no one is watching. Sing like no one is listening. Love like you've never been hurt and live like it's heaven on Earth."

—*Mark Twain*

Fairness

"Injustice anywhere is a threat to justice everywhere."

—*Martin Luther King, Jr.*

Elementary

"When you have eliminated the impossible, that which remains, however improbable, must be the truth."

—*Sir Arthur Conan Doyle*

Wise Words

"Better to remain silent and be thought a fool, than to speak and remove all doubt."

—*Abraham Lincoln*

Indebted

"We do not inherit the earth from our ancestors, we borrow it from our children."

—*Ancient Indian Proverb*

Motivation

"The reward for a thing well done is to have done it."

—*Ralph Waldo Emerson*

My Friend

"I never found a companion that was so companionable as solitude."

—*Henry David Thoreau*

Come to Me

"Happiness is as a butterfly which, when pursued, is always beyond our grasp, but which if you will sit down quietly, may alight upon you."

—*Nathaniel Hawthorne*

Countries

1. NICARAGUA
2. LIECHTENSTEIN
3. DENMARK
4. CANADA
5. AFGHANISTAN

Birds

1. MOCKINGBIRD
2. SPARROW
3. ORIOLE
4. PARAKEET
5. CARDINAL

Kitchen Items

1. CUPBOARD
2. BLENDER
3. REFRIGERATOR
4. STOVE
5. OVEN

Vegetables

1. ARTICHOKE
2. BROCCOLI
3. ASPARAGUS
4. RADISH
5. SPINACH

Airplane

1. ENGINE
2. WING
3. COCKPIT
4. TAIL
5. PILOT

Insects

1. BUTTERFLY
2. DRAGONFLY
3. LADYBUG
4. GRASSHOPPER
5. MOSQUITO

Sports

1. BOXING
2. WRESTLING
3. CRICKET
4. BOWLING
5. VOLLEYBALL

Gems

1. EMERALD
2. OPAL
3. GARNET
4. SAPPHIRE
5. TURQUOISE

Condiments

1. SALT
2. CATSUP
3. MARGARINE
4. MUSTARD
5. HORSERADISH

Dances

1. TWIST
2. WALTZ
3. HUSTLE
4. LIMBO
5. MERENGUE

To Your Health
AN-APPLE-A-DAY-KEEPS-THE-DOCTOR-AWAY.

How Much?
THE-BEST-THINGS-IN-LIFE-ARE-FREE.

Precious
A-MIND-IS-A-TERRIBLE-THING-TO-WASTE.

Missing You
ABSENCE-MAKES-THE-HEART-GROW-FONDER.

Picky
MANY-ARE-CALLED-BUT-FEW-ARE-CHOSEN.

Look Inside
YOU-CAN'T-JUDGE-A-BOOK-BY-ITS-COVER.

Heartbreaker
BETTER-TO-HAVE-LOVED-AND-LOST-THAN-NEVER-TO-HAVE-LOVED-AT-ALL.

Meow
WHEN-THE-CAT'S-AWAY-THE-MICE-WILL-PLAY.

Golden
DO-UNTO-OTHERS-AS-YOU-WOULD-HAVE-THEM-DO-UNTO-YOU.

Imagine That
"If you can dream it, you can do it."
—*Walt Disney*

Age
"A man is not old until regrets take the place of dreams."
—*John Barrymore*

Good Morning
"Early to bed and early to rise, makes a man healthy, wealthy and wise."
—*Benjamin Franklin*

Empty
"One thing only I know, and that is that I know nothing."
—*Socrates*

Be Nice
"No act of kindness, no matter how small, is ever wasted."
—*Aesop*

Order
"A foolish consistency is the hobgoblin of little minds."
—*Emerson*

Happiness
"Men can only be happy when they do not assume that the object of life is happiness."
—*George Orwell*

Highways and Byways
"Two roads diverged in a wood, and I—I took the one less traveled by, and that has made all the difference."
—*Robert Frost*

Deception
"You can fool all the people some of the time, and some of the people all the time, but you cannot fool all the people all the time."
—*Abraham Lincoln*

Glow
"Sometimes your joy is the source of your smile, but sometimes your smile can be the source of your joy."
—*Thich Nhat Hanh*

Chapter 2: Anagrams

Country Singers
1. Johnny Cash
2. Merle Haggard
3. Dolly Parton
4. Garth Brooks
5. Patsy Cline

Baseball Players
1. Babe Ruth
2. Satchel Paige
3. Reggie Jackson
4. Joe DiMaggio
5. Mickey Mantle

Jazz Musicians
1. Count Basie
2. Dave Brubeck
3. Wynton Marsalis
4. Charlie Parker
5. Louis Armstrong

Football Coaches
1. Tom Landry
2. Vince Lombardi
3. Joe Paterno
4. Don Shula
5. Knute Rockne

Fashion World
1. Georgio Armani
2. Calvin Klein
3. Ann Taylor
4. Tommy Hilfiger
5. Liz Claibourne

Astronauts
1. Sally Ride
2. Neil Armstrong
3. Gus Grissom
4. Alan Shepard
5. Buzz Aldrin

Boxers

1. Muhammad Ali
2. Jack Dempsey
3. George Foreman
4. Mike Tyson
5. Jake LaMotta

Scientists

1. Albert Einstein
2. Stephen Hawking
3. Charles Darwin
4. Leonardo da Vinci
5. Isaac Newton

Quarterbacks

1. Roger Staubach
2. Bob Griese
3. Joe Montana
4. Fran Tarkenton
5. Joe Namath

Western Movie Stars

1. Clint Eastwood
2. Roy Rogers
3. John Wayne
4. Chuck Connors
5. Gene Autry

Comedians

1. Billy Crystal
2. Jay Leno
3. Jerry Seinfeld
4. Robin Williams
5. Steve Martin

Mountains

1. Mount Shasta
2. Pikes Peak
3. Mount Everest
4. Matterhorn
5. Grand Teton

Hoosier Cities

1. Evansville
2. Indianapolis
3. Bloomington
4. Lafayette
5. Fort Wayne

Asian Countries

1. Vietnam
2. Thailand
3. South Korea
4. Malaysia
5. Nepal

Lakes

1. Lake Tahoe
2. Lake Superior
3. Great Salt Lake
4. Lake Erie
5. Lake Ontario

California Cities

1. Sacramento
2. Los Angeles
3. San Francisco
4. San Jose
5. San Diego

Islands

1. Greenland
2. Molokai
3. Sumatra
4. Galapagos
5. Martha's Vineyard

Canadian Cities

1. Toronto
2. Montreal
3. Vancouver
4. Calgary
5. Winnipeg

European Countries

1. Germany
2. Spain
3. Austria
4. Switzerland
5. Poland

Space

1. Mars
2. Saturn
3. Uranus
4. Neptune
5. Earth

New England

1. Massachusetts
2. Connecticut
3. Maine
4. New Hampshire
5. Rhode Island

Universities

1. Purdue
2. Notre Dame
3. Georgetown
4. Stanford
5. Penn State

Texas Cities

1. Dallas
2. Houston
3. Austin
4. San Antonio
5. El Paso

Politics

1. The **senator** was found guilty of TREASON.
2. The VOTERS **strove** to impeach him.
3. We should **devote** all of our efforts to getting this bill VETOED.
4. Sometimes the HOLIEST politicians can end up being the most **hostile**.

Rent

1. She was one of the **tannest** TENANTS in the apartment.
2. "Each unit comes with DRAPES," **rasped** the landlord.
3. Don't **worsen** the situation by telling the OWNERS.
4. The house was RENTED with legal **tender**.
5. One more **caveat**: You must VACATE on thirty days' notice.

Toddlers

1. Do not **despair**, your little one will not wear DIAPERS forever!
2. The toddler used MANILA paper to make a toy **animal**.
3. The little **slugger** GURGLES every time he hits the ball.

Insects

1. The HORNET stung the king while he sat on his **throne**.
2. The **unnamed** insect was a rather MUNDANE example of a centipede.
3. The slug sensed DANGER in the **garden**.
4. The **boater** used BORATE to remove the roaches from his yacht.

Art

1. The GALLERY was **largely** responsible for the artist's success.
2. The sculptor's popularity **soared** when the critic said that she ADORES him.
3. **Daniel** NAILED the blue ribbon right onto the artwork.

Food

1. The GREASE in the food **agrees** with him.
2. A **pointer** for your diet: Eat more PROTEIN.
3. He was hired as a TASTER of the bakery's **treats**.

Work

1. The labor is TEDIOUS but he enjoys being **outside**.
2. The workers are **tearing** GRANITE out of the hill.
3. **Andrew** works as a WARDEN.
4. The fireman GLANCED back at the station when the bell **clanged**.
5. The SALESMEN who lost the accounts shall remain **nameless**.

High Seas

1. Even the BLUEST water has a **subtle** hue of green.
2. The **airman** was out of place in the MARINA.
3. He was **hoarse** from shouting at all of the people who went ASHORE.
4. He paddled across the **ocean** in a CANOE.
5. The REEF was kept **free** of trash.

School Rules

1. A CHEATER will be disciplined by the **teacher**.
2. Never **assume** that your chatting AMUSES the teacher.
3. PLEASE do not fall **asleep** during my lecture.
4. The **grader** of the exam will have little REGARD for incomplete answers.

Construction

1. The property has been **zoned** for a DOZEN buildings.
2. As a **general** rule, you will not be able to ENLARGE your house.
3. The **hardest** part was when they TRASHED the building site.
4. He was always **dreaming** of a mansion but built a MIDRANGE house.

Writing

1. He **braved** his teacher's wrath and used an ADVERB instead of an adjective.
2. There is nothing **dopier** than using a PERIOD in the middle of a sentence.
3. She was **editing** a manuscript about DIETING.
4. The **caveman** wrote about the **battle** on his TABLET.

Family Ties

1. She MARRIED her secret **admirer**.
2. The **settler** wrote LETTERS back to his family.
3. Remember when our MOTHERS used to **smother** us with kisses?

Farm

1. **Gosh**, there are a lot of HOGS on a farm!
2. Many of the **framers** of the constitution were also FARMERS.
3. The thirsty HORSE wandered down to the **shore**.

Chapter 3:
What's In a Name?

Gary Player

agar, area, earl, gala, gale, gape, gear, gray, gyre, leap, lyre, page, pale, pare, peal, pear, play, plea, pray, prey, pyre, rage, rape, rare, real, reap, rear, rely, year, yelp

Quincy Jones

cine, coin, cone, cons, cues, eons, ices, icon, inns, ions, jinn, joey, join, joys, neon, nice, nine, none, nose, nosy, noun, nuns, once, ones, onus, sine, sync, yens

Burl Ives

bier, bile, blue, blur, brie, burs, evil, isle, leis, lies, lieu, live, lube, lure, revs, ribs, rile, rise, rive, rube, rubs, rues, rule, ruse, sire, slue, slur, suer, sure, urbs, user, veil, verb, vibe, vier, vies, vile, vise

James Dean

amen, ands, dame, damn, dams, dean, deem, dens, ease, ends, jade, jams, jean, made, mane, mans, mead, mean, mend, mesa, nada, name, need, same, sand, sane, seam, seed, seem, seen, send

Lena Horne

aero, alee, aloe, anon, earl, earn, hale, halo, hare, heal, hear, heel, here, hero, hoar, hoer, hole, hone, horn, lane, lean, leer, loan, lone, lore, near, neon, noel, nona, none, oral, real, reel, roan, role

Helen Hayes

alee, ales, ashy, ayes, ease, easy, eels, else, eyes, hale, hash, hays, heal, heel, hens, lane, lash, lays, lean, leas, lees, lens, leys, nays, sale, sane, seal, seen, shah, shay, slay, yeah, yeas, yens

W. C. Fields

clef, deli, dews, dice, dies, disc, feds, file, fled, flew, iced, ices, ides, idle, isle, leis, lewd, lice, lids, lied, lies, life, self, side, sled, slew, slid, weds, weld, wide, wife, wild, wile, wise

Greta Garbo

abet, aero, agar, agog, area, bare, bate, bear, beat, berg, beta, boar, boat, bore, brag, brat, ergo, gaga, gage, garb, gate, gear, goat, gore, grab, grog, ogre, rage, rare, rate, rear, roar, robe, rote, tare, taro, tear, toga, tore

Jerry Lewis

eels, else, errs, ewer, ewes, eyes, ires, isle, jeer, leer, lees, leis, leys, lies, lyre, reel, rely, rile, rise, ryes, seer, sere, sire, slew, were, wile, wily, wire, wiry, wise, yews

Bear Bryant

abet, ante, area, arty, babe, baby, bane, barb, bare, barn, bate, bean, bear, beat, bent, beta, bran, brat, bray, byte, earn, nary, near, neat, rant, rare, rate, rear, rent, tare, tear, tern, tray, yarn, year

Clark Gable

aback, abler, alack, algae, bagel, bakcr, baler, barge, black, blare, bleak, blear, brace, brake, break, cabal, caber, cable, cager, clear, clerk, creak, gable, glace, glare, grace, label, lacer, lager, large, legal, regal

Evelyn Waugh

angel, angle, eagle, elegy, gavel, glean, gluey, halve, haven, heave, heavy, hyena, laugh, leave, lunge, navel, newel, newly, ulnae, vague, value, vegan, venal, venue, wanly, weave, whale, wheal, wheel

Lauren Bacall

abler, arena, aural, baler, banal, blare, blear, bluer, brace, cabal, caber, cable, calla, canal, clean, clear, crane, cruel, label, lacer, lance, learn, lucre, lunar, renal, ruble, ulcer, ulnae, ulnar, uncle, urban

Lionel Richie

cello, cheer, chili, chill, chino, choir, chore, clone, creel, crone, hello, hence, heron, ichor, icier, ionic, leech, liner, loner, nicer, niche, niece, ocher, ochre, oiler, oriel, recon, relic, rhino

Richard Pryor

acidy, acrid, aphid, ardor, carry, chair, chard, chary, chirp, choir, chord, dairy, diary, hairy, hardy, harpy, harry, hoard, hoary, hydra, hydro, hyoid, ichor, parch, parry, poach, porch, prior, radio, rapid, roach

Jimmy Connors

coins, coons, corns, corny, crony, croon, icons, irons, irony, jimmy, joins, micro, minor, moons, moony, moors, morns, moron, noisy, noons, norms, onion, rooms, roomy, rosin, scion, scorn, scrim, sonic, sonny

John Gielgud

deign, dinge, dingo, dogie, doing, dough, ghoul, glide, glued, going, gouge, guide, guild, guile, hinge, holed, honed, hound, jingo, joule, judge, lined, lingo, lodge, luged, lunge, neigh, nudge, nudie, ogled, oiled, olden, oldie, unled

Alice Walker

alack, alike, awake, aware, calla, clear, clerk, crawl, creak, creek, ileac, ileal, krill, lacer, liker, lilac, relic, waker, wrack, wreak, wreck

Bob Marley

abbey, abler, amber, amble, baler, balmy, belay, beryl, blame, blare, blear, bream, early, labor, lamer, layer, loamy, lobby, maybe, mayor, mealy, molar, moral, moray, realm, relay, royal

Willie Nelson

liens, linen, lines, lions, loins, lolls, neons, newel, nines, noels, noise, sinew, swell, swill, swine, wells, wiles, wills, wines, winos

Tanya Tucker

acuter, arcane, attack, attune, canary, canker, canter, cranky, creaky, curate, cutter, karate, nature, nectar, racket, rattan, recant, retack, tacker, tanker, tantra, tartan, tauter, trance, treaty, truant, tucker, turkey, tyrant, untack

Gore Vidal

derail, dialer, dialog, drivel, galore, gilder, girdle, glared, glider, gloved, glover, goaled, goalie, golder, graved, gravel, gravid, grovel, loader, lodger, ordeal, railed, redial, relaid, reload, roadie, roiled, varied, vialed, voider

Fran Tarkenton

arrant, atoner, errant, errata, fanner, fatten, fatter, karate, nonfat, notate, ornate, rafter, ranker, ranter, rattan, ratter, retorn, retort, rotate, rotten, rotter, tanker, tanner, tantra, tartan, tartar, tarter, tenant

Lionel Richie

choler, cloner, coheir, cohere, coiler, coiner, collie, creole, echoer, encore, enrich, enroll, herein, hereon, heroic, heroin, holier, holler, ironic, lecher, lichen, oilier, recoil, recoin, reline, richen

George Burns

begone, boners, borers, brogue, bugger, bungee, burger, burner, burros, eggers, enrobe, ensure, genres, goners, gorger, gorges, gouger, gouges, greens, grouse, grunge, nurser, rebore, reborn, reruns, resorb, rogues, rouges, rouser, snorer, sourer, suborn, surger, unrobe

Boris Becker

bicker, bikers, borers, briber, bribes, bricks, briers, broker, cobber, corers, corker, creeks, criers, kebobs, recork, resorb, ribber, ribose, ricers, risker, robber, rocker, rosier, scorer, scribe, sicker, sirree, sobber, soiree

Gale Sayers

agrees, argyle, eagles, easels, egress, erases, gasser, geyser, glares, glassy, grassy, grease, greasy, lagers, larges, lasers, layers, leaser, leases, legers, lesser, regale, relays, resale, resays, reseal, sagely, salary, sayers, sealer, serges, slayer

Bill Moyers

beryls, biller, biomes, blimey, boiler, broils, embryo, isomer, libels, limber, limbos, limeys, lories, milers, miller, misery, mobile, morsel, oilers, oriels, rebill, reboil, reoils, ribose, rosily, slimly, smelly, smiler, smiley, solely, somber, sombre, sorely, symbol

Gerald R. Ford

adored, adorer, dodger, fedora, flared, foaled, fodder, folded, folder, forage, forded, forged, forger, galore, glared, goaded, goaled, golder, golfed, golfer, graded, grader, ladder, larded, larder, larger, loaded, loader, loafed, loafer, lodged, lodger, lorded, ordeal, refold, regard, reload, roared, roarer

Ray Charles

archer, arches, archly, arrays, carrel, chaser, cherry, clears, creasy, halers, lacers, lasher, layers, leachy, racers, rarely, rascal, rasher, rashly, relays, sacral, salary, scaler, scarer, sclera, search, sharer, sherry, slayer

John Coltrane

another, cajoler, cartoon, central, channel, chanter, charnel, cheroot, cholera, chorale, chortle, connote, control, coolant, coronal, coronet, enactor, enchant, ethanol, lantern, loather, locater, locator

James Earl Jones

areolas, areoles, armless, arsenal, earless, enamels, enamors, leaners, leasers, loaners, measles, moaners, morsels, nemeses, oarless, oarsman, oarsmen, ransoms, reasons, release, reloans, renames, resales, rescals, resoles, salmons, sealers, senoras, senores, sermons

Ted Williams

dailies, dallies, delimit, details, dilates, dillies, dimwits, distill, elitism, laities, liaised, limited, mallets, malteds, medials, mildest, mildews, millets, misdate, misdeal, misdial, misedit, mislaid, mislead, sallied, sawmill, stalled, stilled, swilled, tallied, tallies, twilled, wallets, wildest, wiliest, willies

Bryant Gumbel

albumen, augment, blarney, blunter, bramble, brambly, bugbear, bumbler, bungler, butlery, buyable, gambler, gambrel, garment, gaunter, gauntly, granule, greatly, grumble, grumbly, mangler, mutable, mutably, nebular, neutral, numeral, tangler, trembly, tumbler, tunable, umbrage

Charlie Parker

airpark, apelike, caliper, caperer, carrier, charier, cheaper, cheapie, chirper, clearer, earache, earlier, hackler, harelip, harrier, heckler, leakier, pealike, percale, perkier, piercer, pricker, prickle, railcar, reacher, replace, replica, replier, reprice

Rod Serling

dineros, dingers, dingoes, droners, eroding, gilders, girders, girdler, girdles, gliders, gloried, glories, godlier, grinder, groined, ignored, ignorer, ignores, ironers, legions, lingers, lingoes, lodgers, lording, lorries, redoing, regilds, regions, regrind, ringers, rosined, singled, slinger, soldier, solider

Carole King

aligner, angelic, calking, calorie, clanger, clangor, clarion, clinger, clinker, coaling, coinage, congeal, corkage, corking, corneal, crinkle, glacier, glancer, grackle, lacking, lankier, larking, leaking, linkage, lockage, locking, oarlike, organic, racking, realign, rocking

Loretta Young

gaunter, gauntly, gloater, glutton, granule, greatly, languor, lottery, lounger, negator, neutral, orangey, oregano, outearn, outrage, outrate, rootlet, tangelo, tangler, taunter, tourney, urology, utterly, younger

Andrew Greeley

angered, dangler, deanery, delayer, derange, drawler, eagerly, enlarge, enraged, eyewear, general, gleaned, gleaner, gnarled, grander, grandly, greened, greener, greenly, grenade, layered, learned, learner, leeward, needler, ragweed, redrawn, regaled, regaler, regrade, relayed, relearn, reneged, reneger, renewal, renewed, renewer, wagered, wagerer, wangled, wangler, wrangle, yearned, yearner

Arthur Godfrey

doughty, drafter, draught, drought, farther, foraged, forager, forayed, forayer, forgery, fraught, frothed, further, garrote, grafted, grafter, grouted, grouter, guarder, gyrated, gyrator, hoarder, hydrate, outdare, outdrag, outhear, outrage, outread, readout, redraft, regraft, roguery, roughed, rougher, toughed, tougher, tragedy, trudger, urethra

Raymond Chandler

alderman, anchored, calendar, chandler, charlady, clamored, clamorer, claymore, colander, cornmeal, crayoned, daydream, deaconry, dormancy, handmade, handyman, handymen, hardcore, headland, heraldry, homeland, manacled, mannerly, modernly, monarchy, normalcy, ordnance, ranchero, ranchman, ranchmen, randomly, romanced, romancer

Eric Dickerson

censored, codeines, coercers, coincide, conceder, concedes, consider, cornered, corniced, cornices, decision, decriers, deerskin, derision, derricks, drinkers, encoders, endorser, nickered, reckoned, reckoner, recocked, recoined, recorked, rednecks, rescored, seconder, sickened, sickener, sincerer

Gabriel García Márquez

acquirer, amicable, arguable, beguiler, biracial, blearier, blurrier, calamari, carriage, cerebral, cerebrum, craggier, creamier, crumbier, embracer, equalize, grimacer, grumbler, imbecile, limberer, lumberer, marriage, quagmire, qualmier, quarrier, queazier, realizer, reburial, requirer, ruralize

Thelonious Monk

emotions, emulsion, hookiest, hooknose, hotlines, hulkiest, hunkiest, huntsmen, insolent, knothole, lookouts, looniest, menthols, mentions, methinks, moleskin, monolith, monotone, moonlets, moonlike, neoliths, noontime, oilstone, outlines, outlooks, outshine, outshone, outsmile, outsmoke, sinkhole, smoothen, smoothie, solution, toilsome, tokenism, unloosen

Alistair Cooke

articles, calories, cloister, colorist, cortisol, costlier, elicitor, isolator, larkiest, locaters, locators, oarlocks, oatcakes, recitals, rockiest, sicklier, silicate, societal, stalkier, stickier, stickler, stockier, tacklers, ticklers, trickles

Alec Guinness

agencies, agenesis, assignee, caginess, classing, cleaning, cleanses, encasing, enlacing, eugenics, euglenas, geniuses, glassine, incenses, issuance, laciness, leanings, leanness, leasings, legacies, licenses, lineages, lunacies, niceness, nuclease, nuisance, salience, sanguine, silences, ugliness, uncasing, unlacing, unseeing, unslings

Oscar Robertson

aborters, ancestor, arrestor, assertor, assorter, baroness, baronets, boasters, boosters, cabooses, cartoons, coarsens, coarsest, coasters, consorts, coronate, coroners, coronets, creators, crooners, crossbar, enac-

tors, reactors, reassort, roasters, roosters, scooters, scorners, senators, snorters, treasons

Abner Doubleday

abounded, adorable, adorably, bearable, bearably, bedaubed, beddable, belauded, bendable, bondable, boneyard, boundary, burdened, burnable, drabbled, duodenal, laboured, oleander, readable, readably, redouble, redubbed, reloaded, reloaned, unbarbed, unbeared, underlay, undoable, unleaded, unloaded, unloader, urbanely

Greg Louganis

aligners, arousing, ganglier, gargling, gasolier, gasoline, gearings,

gigglers, granules, greasing, grousing, grueling, gurgling, laggings, languors, leaguing, leggings, loggings, loungers, nigglers, realigns, regaling, regional, regluing, resoling, seagoing, signaler, singular, slangier, slogging, slugging, snaggier, sugaring

Steve Martin

anisette, emirates, emitters, entreats, estimate, interest, matinees, meatiest, minarets, mistreat, naivetes, nerviest, nitrates, raiments, reinvest, steamier, straiten, teamster, teariest, teatimes, termites, trainees, transmit, treaties, treatise, varmints, vestment, veterans

Chapter 4:
The Meaning of Names

Male Singers

John Denver	Henry John Deutschendorf, Jr.
Ringo Starr	Richard Starkey
Ice-T	Tracy Marrow
Elton John	Reginald Kenneth Dwight
Sting	Gordon Sumner

Female Singers

Joni Mitchell	Roberta Joan Anderson
Tina Turner	Anna Mae Bullock
Patsy Cline	Virginia Patterson Hensley
Billy Holiday	Eleanora Fagan
Dusty Springfield	Mary Isobel Catherine O'Brien

Actors

Alan Alda	Alphonso D'Abruzzo
Martin Sheen	Ramon Estevez
George Burns	Nathan Birnbaum
Gary Cooper	Frank James
Tom Cruise	Thomas Mapother IV

Actresses

Judy Garland	Frances Gumm
Mary Pickford	Gladys Smith
Marilyn Monroe	Norma Jean Baker
Ellen Burstyn	Edna Gilhooley
Rita Hayworth	Margarita Cansino

Sports

Ahmad Rashad	Bobby Moore
Rocky Marciano	Rocco Francis Marchegiano
Kareem Abdul-Jabbar	Ferdinand Lewis Alcindor, Jr.
Hulk Hogan	Terry Gene Bollea
Johnny Bench	Johnny Lee

Pen Names

Lewis Carroll	Charles Lutwidge Dodgson
George Orwell	Eric Arthur Blair
Mark Twain	Samuel Langhorne Clemens
Dr. Seuss	Theodore Geisel
Anthony Burgess	John Wilson

Groups of Birds

Penguins	A colony
Quail	A bevy
Buzzards	A wake
Eagles	A convocation
Larks	An exaltation

Groups of Mammals

Lions	A pride
Oxen	A yoke
Apes	A shrewdness
Ferrets	A business
Hyenas	A clan

Groups of Insects

Flies	A business
Locusts	A plague
Grasshoppers	A cloud
Cockroaches	An intrusion
Ants	A colony

Animal Adjectives

Ass	Asinine
Bee	Apian
Bird	Avian
Bull	Taurine
Cat	Feline

Female Names

Deer	Doe
Ferret	Hob
Donkey	Jenny
Elephant	Cow
Lobster	Hen

Male Names

Pigeon	Cock
Bison	Bull
Horse	Stallion
Pig	Boar
Turkey	Gobbler

Offspring

Moose	Calf
Cougar	Kitten
Goat	Kid
Kangaroo	Joey
Ostrich	Chick

To Your Health

Dermatophobia	Fear of skin disease
Cardiophobia	Fear of heart disease
Pathophobia	Fear of disease
Iatrophobia	Fear of going to the doctor
Emetophobia	Fear of vomiting

Insects and Animals

Arachnophobia	Fear of spiders
Ichthyophobia	Fear of fish
Ornithophobia	Fear of birds
Herpetophobia	Fear of reptiles
Apiophobia	Fear of bees

Don't Go Outside

Aerophobia	Fear of fresh air
Lunaphobia	Fear of the moon
Noctiphobia	Fear of the night
Limnophobia	Fear of lakes
Chinophobia	Fear of snow

Other People

Androphobia	Fear of men
Venustraphobia	Fear of beautiful women
Pedophobia	Fear or dislike of children
Harpaxophobia	Fear of robbers
Ochlophobia	Fear of crowds

Objects

Crystallophobia	Fear of glass
Bacillophobia	Fear of missiles
Bibliophobia	Fear of books
Cyberphobia	Fear of computers
Mechanophobia	Fear of machinery

Latin Names for Trees

Populus grandidentata	Bigtooth aspen
Ulmus rubra	Red elm
Acer rubrum	Red maple
Acer saccharum	Sugar maple
Juniperus virginiana	Eastern red cedar

Medical Names for Body Parts

Popliteal	Hollow in back of knee
Hallux	Big toe
Sclera	White of eye
Vomer	Slender bone between nostrils
Pollex	Thumb

Occupation Names

Wright	One who repairs things
Webster	Operates looms
Sawyer	Sawer of wood
Mason	Bricklayer
Glazier	Window glassman

Names for Colors

Azure	Sky blue
Russet	Reddish brown
Saffron	Orange yellow
Glaucous	Sea green
Mauve	Violet

Names for Measurements

Decibel	Unit for sound intensity
Parsec	Unit of interstellar distance
Dyne	Unit of force
Fathom	Unit used to measure depth of water
Megadeath	Unit of fatality

Doctrines (-ism)

Accidentalism	Theory that events do not have causes
Hedonism	Belief that pleasure is the main goal in life
Solipsism	Theory that self-existence is the only certainty
Optimism	A doctrine that this is the best possible world
Theism	Belief in the existence of God

Government (-cracy)

Democracy	Government by the people
Meritocracy	Government selected by ability
Paedocracy	Government by children
Aristocracy	Government by the nobility
Theocracy	Government by divine guidance

Divination (-mancy)

Necromancy	Divination by conjuring up the dead
Crystallomancy	Divination by gazing into a reflective object
Bibliomancy	Divination by opening a book at random
Ichthyomancy	Divination by looking at fish entrails
Gyromancy	Divination by walking in a circle until dizzy

Obsessions (-mania)

Xenomania	Obsession with foreign things
Bibliomania	Obsession with books
Kleptomania	Obsession with stealing
Megalomania	Obsession with grandiose behavior
Egomania	Obsession with yourself

Sciences (-ology)

Biology	Study of life
Hypnology	Study of sleep
Kinesiology	Study of human movement
Ecology	Study of the environment
Graphology	Study of handwriting

Shapes (-form)

Boviform	Ox-shaped
Reniform	Kidney-shaped
Cuneiform	Wedge-shaped
Stelliform	Star-shaped
Guttiform	Drop-shaped

Knowledge (-osophy)

Misosophy	Hatred of knowledge
Philosophy	Science of knowledge
Anthroposophy	Knowledge of human development
Ontosophy	Knowledge of being
Pansophy	Universal knowledge

Feeding (-orous)

Insectivorous	Feeding on insects
Carnivorous	Feeding on animals
Granivorous	Feeding on grain
Baccivorous	Feeding on berries
Panivorous	Feeding on bread

Lovers (-phile)

Bibliophile	Lover of books
Audiophile	Lover of high-fidelity sound
Sinophile	Lover of China and Chinese culture
Hippophile	Lover of horses
Theophile	Lover of God

Polygons (-gon)

Hexagon	Polygon with six sides
Isagon	Polygon whose angles are equal
Dodecagon	Polygon with twelve sides
Quindecagon	Polygon with fifteen sides
Nonagon	Polygon with nine sides

Chapter 5: Logogriphs

Behead to Make H Words
1. shades and hades
2. wheel and heel
3. chives and hives
4. thorns and horns

Behead to Make C Words
1. screws and crews
2. acorn and corn
3. icon and con
4. scent and cent

Behead to Make P Words
1. spit and pit
2. space and pace
3. spike and pike
4. open and pen
5. opal and pal

Behead to Make A Words
1. lace and ace
2. haunt and aunt
3. wart and art
4. farm and arm
5. ranger and anger

Behead to Make U Words
1. bunion and union
2. pusher and usher
3. pump and ump

Behead to Make T Words
1. strip and trip
2. atoll and toll
3. stick and tick
4. star and tar
5. atom and tom

Behead to Make L Words
1. flight and light
2. blink and link
3. glove and love
4. flab and lab
5. clip and lip

Behead to Make R Words

1. driver and river
2. drink and rink
3. broach and roach
4. crib and rib
5. crook and rook

Behead to Make E Words

1. beast and east
2. welder and elder
3. terror and error
4. devil and evil

Behead to Make I Words

1. pirate and irate
2. tissue and issue
3. oink and ink
4. mice and ice
5. finch and inch

Curtail These M Words

1. mate and mat
2. median and media
3. moon and moo
4. menu and men
5. mad and ma

Curtail These B Words

1. bank and ban
2. beer and bee
3. belly and bell
4. board and boar
5. brand and bran

Curtail These H Words

1. hate and hat
2. harem and hare
3. hazel and haze

Curtail These D Words

1. dock and doc
2. doer and doe
3. dent and den
4. debt and Deb

Curtail These S Words

1. sumo and sum
2. slate and slat
3. slope and slop
4. soda and sod
5. seat and sea

Curtail These K Words

1. kite and kit
2. king and kin
3. keno and Ken

Curtail These G Words

1. goof and goo
2. grind and grin
3. gripe and grip
4. grade and grad
5. gash and gas

Curtail These C Words

1. cube and Cub
2. cone and con
3. chump and chum
4. closet and close
5. chin and chi

Syncopate These L Words

1. latte and late
2. launch and lunch
3. lever and leer
4. lice and lie
5. loft and lot

Syncopate These T Words

1. thread and tread
2. trail and tail
3. title and tile
4. tone and toe

Syncopate These D Words

1. dome and doe
2. dread and dead
3. donor and door

Syncopate These P Words

1. pump and pup
2. play and pay
3. post and pot

Syncopate These S Words

1. slaw and saw
2. shake and sake
3. shell and sell
4. shelf and self
5. slum and sum

Syncopate These B Words

1. baby and bay
2. bait and bat
3. bend and bed
4. black and back

Syncopate These W Words

1. wing and wig
2. work and wok
3. writhe and write

Syncopate These R Words

1. ramp and rap
2. rugby and ruby
3. role and roe
4. ridge and ride

Transadd This Word: Retain

1. certain
2. strainer
3. painter
4. latrine
5. hairnet

Transadd This Word: Horse

1. ashore
2. chores
3. herons
4. hordes

Transadd This Word: Teach
1. chalet
2. sachet
3. cachet

Transadd This Word: Cereal
1. cleaver
2. declare
3. replace
4. treacle
5. cleaner

Transadd This Word: Earth
1. bather
2. hatter
3. father
4. halter

Transadd This Word: Lace
1. cable
2. cleat
3. camel
4. decal

Transadd This Word: Star
1. brats
2. rates
3. rafts
4. carts

Transadd This Word: Love
1. vowel
2. novel
3. solve
4. olive

Chapter 6: Word Ladders

PIG to STY
PIG, WIG, WAG, WAY, SAY, STY

SAD to JOY
SAD, SOD, SOY, JOY

FOG to SUN
FOG, BOG, BUG, BUN, SUN

OWL to FOX
OWL, OIL, NIL, NIX, FIX, FOX

JOG to RUN
JOG, JUG, RUG, RUN

OLD to NEW
OLD, ODD, ADD, AID, BID, BED, FED, FEW, NEW

ICE to HOT
ICE, ACE, AYE, DYE, DOE, HOE, HOT

ONE to TWO
ONE, OLE, ALE, AYE, DYE, DOE, TOE, TOO, TWO

TOP to END
TOP, BOP, BOD, BID, AID, AND, END

ARM to LEG
ARM, ARE, AYE, LYE, LEE, LEG

JET to FLY
JET, PET, PAT, PAY, PLY, FLY

DRY to WET
DRY, PRY, PAY, PAT, PET, WET

PAL to FOE
PAL, PAR, FAR, FOR, FOE

NEW to OLD
NEW, DEW, DEN, DIN, DID, AID, ADD, ODD, OLD

FOUR to FIVE
FOUR, FOUL, FOOL, FOOT, FORT, FORE, FIRE, FIVE

SAND to DUNE
SAND, SANK, SUNK, DUNK, DUNE

WILD to TAME
WILD, MILD, MILE, TILE, TALE, TAME

HATE to LOVE
HATE, HAVE, HOVE, LOVE

WARM to COLD
WARM, WORM, WORD, CORD, COLD

SEED to TREE
SEED, FEED, FLED, FLEE, FREE, TREE

MORE to LESS
MORE, LORE, LOSE, LOSS, LESS

FOOL to WISE
FOOL, POOL, POLL, PILL, WILL, WILE, WISE

GRUB to WORM
GRUB, GRAB, GRAD, GOAD, LOAD, LORD, WORD, WORM

DAYS to YEAR
DAYS, BAYS, BOYS, BOAS, BOAR, BEAR, YEAR

BORN to FREE
BORN, TORN, TERN, TEEN, THEN, THEE, TREE, FREE

PAWN to KING
PAWN, PAWS, PANS, PINS, PING, KING

SEED to LAWN
SEED, SEES, SEWS, SAWS, LAWS, LAWN

HAND to FOOT
HAND, BAND, BOND, FOND, FOOD, FOOT

HEAT to FIRE
HEAT, HEAD, HERD, HERE, HIRE, FIRE

WORD to GAME

WORD, CORD, CARD, CARE, CAME, GAME

WHEAT to BREAD

WHEAT, CHEAT, CLEAT, BLEAT, BLEAK, BREAK, BREAD

SNACK to MEALS

SNACK, STACK, STARK, STARS, SEARS, SEALS, MEALS

FLESH to BLOOD

FLESH, FLASH, FLASK, FLANK, BLANK, BLAND, BLOND, BLOOD

BABES to WOODS

BABES, BARES, WARES, WARDS, WORDS, WOODS

NORTH to SOUTH

NORTH, FORTH, FORTS, SORTS, SOOTS, SOOTH, SOUTH

FRESH to STALE

FRESH, FLESH, FLASH, FLASK, FLACK, SLACK, STACK, STALK, STALE

SHARP to BLUNT

SHARP, SHARE, SPARE, SPARS, SPURS, SLURS, BLURS, BLURT, BLUNT

TEARS to SMILE

TEARS, SEARS, STARS, STARE, STALE, STILE, SMILE

SMILE to FROWN

SMILE, SMITE, SPITE, SPITS, SLITS, SLOTS, SLOWS, FLOWS, FLOWN, FROWN

SLEEP to DREAM

SLEEP, BLEEP, BLEED, BREED, BREAD, DREAD, DREAM

Chapter 7: Acrostics

Reservations
1. Ticket
2. Road
3. Airline
4. Vacation
5. Excursion
6. Luggage
* **TRAVEL**

May Flowers
1. Season
2. Plant
3. Rain
4. Insect
5. New
6. Garden
* **SPRING**

The Final Frontier
1. Stars
2. Planet
3. Asteroids
4. Comet
5. Extraterrestrial
* **SPACE**

Beginning to Look a Lot Like
1. Chestnuts
2. Halls
3. Ribbons
4. Icicle
5. Stockings
6. Toys
7. Mouse
8. Angels
9. Snow
* **CHRISTMAS**

Earth Plot
1. Grow
2. Asparagus
3. Radish
4. Dig

5. Earth
6. Nature
* **GARDEN**

Baby
1. Innocent
2. Nap
3. Food
4. Amused
5. New
6. Toddler
* **INFANT**

Knowledge
1. Lesson
2. Education
3. Arithmetic
4. Reading
5. Notes
* **LEARN**

Athletics
1. Stadium
2. Practice
3. Overhead
4. Race
5. Track
6. Score
* **SPORTS**

Summer Fun
1. Backyard
2. Ashes
3. Roast
4. Beef
5. Eat
6. Cookout
7. Utensils
8. Ember
* **BARBECUE**

Sewing
1. NovelisT
2. EpitapH
3. EquatoR

4. DarE
5. LaurA
6. EarneD
* **NEEDLE, THREAD**

Wedding Bells
1. BakinG
2. ReadeR
3. IgloO
4. DiscO
5. EnthusiasM
* **BRIDE, GROOM**

Assignment
1. HoW
2. OrlandO
3. MajoR
4. EarmarK
* **HOME WORK**

Doing One Now
1. WinG
2. OkrA
3. RandoM
4. DefinE
* **WORD GAME**

Four-Leaf Clover
1. LyriC
2. UtaH
3. CharismA
4. KisseR
5. YaM
* **LUCKY CHARM**

Defraud
1. SemiautomatiC
2. TougH
3. EmpirE
4. AntarcticA
5. LawsuiT
* **STEAL, CHEAT**

On the Silver Screen
1. MatineeS
2. OutfiT
3. VisA
4. InterioR
5. ExtraS
* **MOVIE STARS**

Cumulonimbus
1. SporadiC
2. TropicaL
3. OntariO
4. RousseaU
5. MilD
* **STORM CLOUD**

What a Racket
1. TriviA
2. ExhibitioN
3. NastY
4. NemO
5. InspiratioN
6. ServE
* **TENNIS, ANYONE?**

Composition
1. PavloV
2. OctavE
3. EaR
4. ManuscriptS
5. SatirE
* **POEMS, VERSE**

Captive
1. Grass
2. Always
3. Greener
4. Side
Saying: The grass is always greener on the other side.
Acrostic: GAGS

Abbreviated Part of an Hour
1. Mother
2. Invention
3. Necessity
Saying: Necessity is the mother of invention.
Acrostic: MIN

Automatons Abbreviated
1. Bitten
2. Once
3. Twice
4. Shy
Saying: Once bitten, twice shy.
Acrostic: BOTS

Overnight Water
1. Dear
2. Elementary
3. Watson
Saying: Elementary, my dear Watson.
Acrostic: DEW

Auction Offer
1. Bucket
2. In
3. Drop
Saying: A drop in the bucket.
Acrostic: BID

Me and You
1. Better
2. One
3. Two
4. Heads
Saying: Two heads are better than one.
Acrostic: BOTH

Organized Crime Gang
1. Moon
2. Once
3. Blue
Saying: Once in a blue moon.
Acrostic: MOB

Up-Down Toy
1. You
2. Only
3. Young
4. Once

Saying: You are only young once.
Acrostic: YOYO

Auto
1. Customer
2. Always
3. Right

Saying: The customer is always right.
Acrostic: CAR

Not Good
1. Bite
2. Another
3. Dust

Saying: Another one bites the dust.
Acrostic: BAD

Chapter 8: Inside Words

Buildings
hot+el=hotel
pal+ace=palace
off+ice=office

At School
tea+cher=teacher
hi+story=history
less+on=lesson

Bird Watching
rob+in=robin
pig+eon=pigeon
spar+row=sparrow

In the Water
oct+opus=octopus
her+ring=herring
min+now=minnow

On the Land
pant+her=panther
don+key=donkey
stall+ion=stallion

Many Moods
am+used=amused
con+tent=content
curio+us=curious

World Cities
cam+bridge=Cambridge
chic+ago=Chicago
par+is=Paris

Plants
car+nation=carnation
lot+us=lotus
we+ed=weed

Around the House
was+her=washer
pill+ow=pillow
pan+try=pantry

Chicken Parts
feat+her=feather
he+art=heart
bra+in=brain

U.S. Presidents
1. Carter, art
2. Washington, ash
3. Clinton, lint

Wildlife
1. spider, pi
2. shrimp, rim
3. crocodile, cod

Vegetables
1. cabbage, bag
2. spinach, pin
3. asparagus, par

Drink Up
1. martini, tin
2. Manhattan, hat
3. screwdriver, crew

Colors
1. white, hit
2. brown, row
3. orange, rang

Games
1. bridge, id
2. dominoes, no
3. checkers, heck

Dog Breeds
1. boxer, ox
2. terrier, err
3. dachshund, shun

Plants
1. clover, love
2. pumpkin, ump
3. dandelion, deli

Careers
1. model, ode
2. executive, cut
3. secretary, tar

Edible
1. marshmallow, mall
2. tomato, mat
3. vanilla, nil

Sequence: PST
campstool, capstan, capstone, chopstick, chopsticks, dipstick, dripstone, dumpster, hipster, jumpstart, lipstick, quipster, slapstick, slipstream, soapstone, sweepstake, sweepstakes, tipster, topstitch, upstage, upstairs, upstanding, upstart, upstate, upstream, upstroke, whipstitch

Sequence: YMN
gymnasium, gymnasiums, gymnast, gymnastic, gymnastically, gymnastics, gymnosperm, hymn, hymnal, hymnbook, hymned, hymning, hymnist, hymns

Sequence: THM
algorithm, algorithmic, arithmetic, arithmetical, arithmetically, arithmetician, arrhythmia, arrhythmic, asthma, asthmatic, bequeathment, betrothment, biorhythm, birthmark, dysrhythmia, earthmover, ethmoid, ethmoidal, eurhythmics, isthmus, isthmuses, logarithm, logarithmic, logarithmically, mythmaker, northman, northmen, northmost, rhythm, rhythmic, rhythmical, rhythmically, southmost

Sequence: NVA
canvas, canvasback, canvass, canvassed, canvasser, canvassing, convalesce, convalesced, convalescence, convalescent, convalescing, invade, invaded, invader, invading, invalid, invalidate, invalidated, invalidating, invalidation, invalidism, invalidity, invaluable, invaluableness, invaluably, invariability, invariable, invariableness, invariably, invariance, invariant, invasion, invasive, invasiveness, noninvasive, nonvascular, unvaccinated, unvalued, unvanquishable, unvanquished, unvariable, unvaried, unvariedness, unvarnished, unvarying

Sequence: NLA
enlarge, enlarged, enlargement, enlarger, enlarging, inlaid, inland, inlay, inlayer, inlaying, mainland, sunlamp, unlabeled, unlabored, unlace, unlaced, unladylike, unla-

mented, unlash, unlatch, unlatched, unlawful, unlawfully, unlawfulness, vacationland

Sequence: IZZ
blizzard, dizzily, dizziness, dizzy, dizzying, drizzle, drizzled, drizzling, drizzly, fizz, fizzed, fizzing, fizzle, fizzled, fizzling, fizzy, frizz, frizzed, frizzes, frizzing, frizzy, gizzard, grizzle, grizzled, grizzly, mizzen, mizzenmast, pizza, pizzazz, pizzeria, quizzed, quizzer, quizzical, quizzically, quizzing, sizzle, sizzled, sizzler, sizzling, swizzle, tizzy, whizzed, whizzing

Sequence: GGA
baggage, beggar, beggared, beggaring, beggarliness, beggarly, beggars, beggary, braggadocio, braggart, haggard, haggardly, laggard, luggage, niggard, niggardliness, niggardly, reggae, sluggard, toboggan, tobogganing, tobogganist

Sequence: FFU
coiffure, diffuse, diffused, diffusely, diffuseness, diffuser, diffusing, diffusion, diffusive, diffusively, diffusiveness, diffusivity, effulgence, effulgent, effuse, effused, effusing, effusion, effusive, effusively, effusiveness, suffuse, suffused, suffusing, suffusion

Sequence: DUA
dual, dualism, dualist, dualistic, duality, gradual, gradualism, graduality, gradually, gradualness, graduate, graduated, graduating, graduation, graduator, individual, individualism, individualist, individualistic, individualistically, individuality, individualization, individualize,

individualized, individually, individuals, individuate, individuation, postgraduate, residual, residuals, residuary, undergraduate

Sequence: CKH
backhand, backhanded, backhander, backhaul, backhoe, backhouse, blackhead, blockhead, blockheaded, blockhouse, buckhound, chuckhole, cockhorse, deckhand, deckhouse, dockhand, jackhammer, muckheap, packhorse, stockholder, stockholders, stockholding, thickhead, thickheaded

Beware of Liposuction
tulip, maple, oak
(A Timbuk**[tu lip]**osuction can cause asth**[ma. Ple]**nty of people in Gen**[oa k]**now this already.)

Food Fit
trumpet, tuba, violin
(He threw a tan**[trum, pet]**rified that the **[tub a]**ctually contained ra**[violi n]**oodles.)

Problem Child
Saturn, Venus, Mars
(Li**[sa turn]**s away e**[ven us]**. She only talks to her friends in gram**[mar s]**chool.)

Stuntman
carrot, spinach, potato
(As the **[car rot]**ated rapidly, the **[spin ach]**ieved Jimmy a s**[pot ato]**p the daredevil hall of fame.)

Whirlwind
dog, rabbit, cat
(She watched the torna**[do g][rab bits]** of the repli**[ca t]**hat were loose.)

Bob
1. bobcat
2. bobby
3. bobtail
4. bobby socks
5. bobsled

Jack
1. jackpot
2. flapjack
3. hijack
5. lumberjack

Tom
1. tomboy
2. tomcat
3. tomfool
4. tomahawk

Mary
1. primary
2. Maryland
3. rosemary
4. customary

Jim
1. jim-dandy
2. jimmy
3. jimsonweed
4. jimmies

Bill
1. billfold
2. hillbilly
3. handbill
4. billy
5. playbill

Chapter 9: Missing Pieces

For the Birds
1. A bird in the hand is worth two in the bush.
2. Kill two birds with one stone.
3. The early bird catches the worm.

Equestrian
1. I'm so hungry I could eat a horse.
2. Don't put the cart before the horse.
3. You can lead a horse to water, but you can't make him drink.

Time
1. Time and tides wait for no man.
2. Time heals all wounds.
3. A stitch in time saves nine.

In the Family
1. Like father, like son.
2. Blood is thicker than water.
3. Necessity is the mother of invention.

Career Advice
1. All work and no play makes Jack a dull boy.
2. Nothing ventured, nothing gained.
3. If at first you don't succeed, try, try again.

Love Advice
1. Absence makes the heart grow fonder.
2. It takes two to tango.
3. Beauty is in the eye of the beholder.

Landscape
1. The grass is always greener on the other side of the fence.
2. A rolling stone gathers no moss.
3. Making a mountain out of a molehill.

Timely Advice
1. Better late than never.
2. Never put off until tomorrow what you can do today.
3. Strike while the iron is hot.

Poultry
1. Don't count your chickens before they hatch.
2. Birds of a feather flock together.
3. Don't put all your eggs in one basket.

In the Kitchen
1. Too many cooks spoil the broth.
2. Out of the frying pan into the fire.
3. If you can't stand the heat, get out of the kitchen.

Lacking
1. A friend in need is a friend indeed.
2. Beggars can't be choosers.
3. Finders keepers, losers weepers.

Nature
1. Still waters run deep.
2. When the cat's away, the mice will play.
3. You reap what you sow.

Words
1. One picture is worth a thousand words.
2. Actions speak louder than words.
3. A word to the wise.

Wheel Around
1. The squeaky wheel gets the grease.
2. What goes around comes around.
3. Don't put the cart before the horse.

Force
1. United we stand, divided we fall.
2. Might makes right.
3. Fools rush in where angels fear to tread.

Abbreviated Cinema Challenge 1

Forrest Gump
Starring Tom Hanks, Robin Wright Penn, and Gary Sinise.

Abbreviated Cinema Challenge 2

Titanic
Starring Leonardo DiCaprio and Kate Winslet.

Abbreviated Cinema Challenge 3

Pulp Fiction
Starring John Travolta, Samuel L. Jackson, and Uma Thurman.

Abbreviated Cinema Challenge 4

Raiders of the Lost Ark
Starring Harrison Ford, Karen Allen, and Paul Freeman.

Abbreviated Cinema Challenge 5

Apocalypse Now
Starring Marlon Brando, Robert Duvall, and Martin Sheen.

Abbreviated Cinema Challenge 6

Star Wars
Starring Mark Hamill, Harrison Ford, Carrie Fisher, and Alec Guinness.

Abbreviated Cinema Challenge 7

Taxi Driver
Starring Robert De Niro, Cybill Shepherd, Jodie Foster, and Harvey Keitel.

Abbreviated Cinema Challenge 8

The Godfather
Starring Marlon Brando, Al Pacino, James Caan, and Robert Duvall.

Abbreviated Cinema Challenge 9

To Kill a Mockingbird
Starring Gregory Peck, Robert Duvall, and Brock Peters.

Abbreviated Cinema Challenge 10

Singin' in the Rain
Starring Gene Kelly, Donald O'Connor, and Debbie Reynolds.

Abbreviated Cinema Challenge 11

It's a Wonderful Life
Starring James Stewart, Donna Reed, and Lionel Barrymore.

Abbreviated Cinema Challenge 12

Casablanca
Starring Humphrey Bogart and Ingrid Bergman.

Abbreviated Cinema Challenge 13

Citizen Kane
Starring Orson Welles and Joseph Cotten.

Abbreviated Cinema Challenge 14

Gone with the Wind
Starring Vivien Leigh and Clark Gable.

Red, White, and Blue

- 50 States = Unites States of America
- Great Lakes = Superior, Huron, Erie, Ontario, Michigan
- 13 Original Colonies = Massachusetts, Rhode Island, Connecticut, New Hampshire, New York, Delaware, New Jersey, Pennsylvania, Virginia, Maryland, North Carolina, South Carolina, Georgia

Lists

- North, South, East, West = Compass Points
- John, Paul, George, Ringo = Beatles
- U, O, I, E, A = Vowels

Story Time

- 7 Dwarfs = Grumpy, Doc, Bashful, Sleepy, Sneezy, Happy, Dopey
- Santa's Reindeer = Dasher, Dancer, Prancer, Vixen, Comet, Cupid, Donner, Blitzen
- 3 Bears = Mama Bear, Papa Bear, Baby Bear

Sports

- 100 Yards = 1 Football Field
- 52 Cards = 1 Deck
- 18 Holes = 1 Golf Course

For Good Measure

- 12 Inches = 1 Foot
- 360 Degrees = 1 Circle
- 3 Feet = 1 Yard

Color and Composition

- 1 Picture = 1,000 Words
- Blue + Red + Yellow = Primary Colors
- 1 Square = 4 Sides

Time
- 7 Days = 1 Week
- 12 Months = 1 Year
- Monday, Tuesday, Wednesday, Thursday, Friday = Weekdays

Makes Sense
- 100 Cents = 1 Dollar
- Penny Saved = Penny Earned
- 2 Quarters + 3 Nickels = 65 Pennies

Chapter 10: Triplets

Within the Mattress
SPRING: spring chicken, offspring, springboard
bedspring

School Assignment
HOME: homemade, nursing home, homespun
homework

Dust Guard
SLIP: pink slip, slipknot, slipstream
slipcover

Sewage Disposal
TANK: gas tank, tank top, think tank
septic tank

Elevated Fort
TREE: Christmas tree, treetop, tree-hugger
tree house

Hourglass
EGG: goose egg, egg white, egghead
egg timer

Light in Flight
FLY: fly ball, butterfly, dragonfly
firefly

Ocean Boundary
LINE: deadline, lineman, hairline
coastline

Farm Fence with a Twist
WIRE: haywire, wire service, hotwire
barbed wire

A Plant with Edible Fruit
BLUE: bluegrass, baby blue, bluebird
blueberry

An Overwhelming Victory
LAND: heartland, landlord, mainland
landslide

A Speedy Bird
ROAD: railroad, road rage, roadkill
roadrunner

Football Helmet Front
FACE: boldface, poker face, face card
facemask

Heavy Metal Toss
SHOT: big shot, gunshot, long shot
shot put

Hoops
BALL: mothball, ballpoint, ballroom
basketball

Boxing Victory
KNOCK: knockdown, knock-knee, knockoff
knockout

Race Refueling
STOP: stopgap, stopwatch, shortstop
pit stop

Football Leader
BACK: drawback, backspace, horseback
quarterback

Rouse the Troops
TALK: talk show, sweet talk, talk shop
pep talk

Internet Maintainer
MASTER: mastermind, grand master, masterpiece
webmaster

TV—with Prizes
GAME: word game, fair game, game plan
game show

Info Delivered to Your Door
PAPER: paperback, sandpaper, paper-thin
newspaper

TV Forecaster
WEATHER: weathervane, fair-weather, weatherproof
weatherman

Price Reduction
MARK: hallmark, postmark, bookmark
markdown

Paper Money
NOTE: footnote, notebook, keynote
banknote

Greeting or Agreement
SHAKE: milkshake, shakedown, shakeup
handshake

Farmer's Tool
PITCH: sales pitch, pitch dark, fever pitch
pitchfork

The Presiding Officer
CHAIR: chairlift, highchair, armchair
chairman

Office Pen

POINT: checkpoint, needlepoint, point blank

ballpoint

County Fair Fare

DOG: top dog, doghouse, dog tag

hotdog

Illegal Whiskey

MOON: blue moon, honeymoon, moonstruck

moonshine

A Common Quantity of Beer

PACK: packhorse, backpack, fanny pack,

six-pack

After Heavy Drinking

OVER: overcast, once-over, over-drive

hangover

Pool Protector

LIFE: still life, lifestyle, wildlife

lifeguard

Mechanic

MONKEY: monkey bars, monkey business, monkey wrench

grease monkey

Man in the Armed Forces

SERVICE: answering service, Secret Service, service charge

serviceman

Movie Author

SCREEN: smokescreen, sunscreen, silkscreen

screenwriter

Chapter 11: Inky Pinkys

Animals
1. drab crab
2. male whale
3. ape cape

All Wet
1. rain stain
2. snake lake
3. damp camp

This and That
1. ear year
2. brook book
3. peas please

Yummy
1. sweet treat
2. snack shack
3. fake cake

Mammals
1. rare mare
2. bear hair
3. cheap sheep

Hygiene
1. clean teen
2. weird beard
3. bath path

Wildlife
1. shark park
2. free bee
3. fat cat

Nonverbal Communication
1. half laugh
2. brave wave
3. neck peck

Work
1. paid maid
2. wage rage
3. brain drain

Transportation
1. space race
2. star car
3. large barge

Sports
1. track shack
2. dream team
3. small ball

Includes an S Word
1. fleet street
2. smart start
3. salt vault

Around the House
1. flag bag
2. dame frame
3. spare chair

Animal Life
1. nest pest
2. mice dice
3. quick chick

Things People Do
1. brief thief
2. zoo crew
3. yard guard

Apparel
1. shirt dirt
2. chess dress
3. flat hat

Colorful Food
1. tan bran
2. green bean
3. blue brew

Odds and Ends
1. red thread
2. swell bell
3. thick stick

Shopping

1. small mall
2. swift gift
3. pie buy

Body Functions

1. deep sleep
2. ear fear
3. Swiss kiss

Family

1. glad dad
2. wild child
3. mouse house

Manmade

1. wet jet
2. big dig
3. vain train

Small Change

1. dime crime
2. nurse purse
3. nice price

The Great Outdoors

1. mountain fountain
2. forest florist
3. wonder thunder

Anthropomorphize

1. wiser geyser
2. wizard lizard
3. witty kitty

Sports World

1. jockey hockey
2. soccer locker
3. richer pitcher

B Word Included

1. better sweater
2. plumper bumper
3. beaver fever

Odd Occupations

1. summer plumber
2. gutter cutter
3. scooter tutor

Personal Descriptions

1. snoozer loser
2. tire buyer
3. finer diner

By the Numbers

1. midget digit
2. nickel pickle
3. dirty thirty

Chapter 12: Homophone Fun

Homophone Pair Challenge 1

1. banned band
2. hoarse horse
3. stair stare

Homophone Pair Challenge 2

1. sail sale
2. weak week
3. thyme time

Homophone Pair Challenge 3

1. towed toad
2. fair fare
3. prince prints

Homophone Pair Challenge 4

1. peddle pedal
2. night knight
3. dear deer

Homophone Pair Challenge 5

1. idle idol
2. ant aunt
3. mourning morning

Homophone Pair Challenge 6

1. ore oar
2. write right
3. coarse course

Homophone Pair Challenge 7

1. main mane
2. heal heel
3. sweet suite

Homophone Pair Challenge 8

1. carrot karat
2. border boarder
3. chilly chili

Homophone Pair Challenge 9

1. prophet profit
2. sun son
3. current currant

Homophone Pair Challenge 10

1. pale pail
2. toe tow
3. cantor canter

Homophone Pair Challenge 11

1. sore soar
2. bored board
3. whale wail

Homophone Pair Challenge 12

1. wine whine
2. serial cereal
3. lone loan

Homophone Pair Challenge 13

1. steal steel
2. close clothes
3. bare bear

Homophone Pair Challenge 14

1. tense tents
2. heard herd
3. foul fowl

Homophone Pair Challenge 15
1. cash cache
2. meet meat
3. bolder boulder

Homophone Pair Challenge 16
1. hostile hostel
2. maize maze
3. minor miner

Homophone Pair Challenge 17
1. wholly holy
2. hare hair
3. claws clause

Homophone Pair Challenge 18
1. whole hole
2. male mail
3. tacks tax

Homophone Pair Challenge 19
1. cymbal symbol
2. mince mints
3. bridal bridle

Homophone Pair Challenge 20
1. cellar seller
2. better bettor
3. cedar seeder

Basketball
1. Karl Malone
2. Larry Bird
3. Phil Jackson

Trees
1. pine
2. maple
3. cedar

United
1. Kansas
2. Michigan
3. New Mexico

Fine Wine
1. Burgundy
2. Cabernet
3. Chardonnay

Authors
1. Edgar Allan Poe
2. Mark Twain
3. Stephen King

Reptiles
1. alligator
2. lizard
3. chameleon

Stars
1. Dudley Moore
2. Lon Chaney
3. Marilyn Monroe

Birds
1. heron
2. cardinal
3. eagle

Movies
1. Lion King
2. Sweet Home Alabama
3. Ocean's Eleven

Television
1. Jeopardy
2. All My Children
3. Fraiser

Chapter 13: Dictionary Fun

Spelling Challenge 1
accidentally

Spelling Challenge 2
maneuver

Spelling Challenge 3
separate

Spelling Challenge 4
potato

Spelling Challenge 5
camouflage

Spelling Challenge 6
definite

Spelling Challenge 7
bargain

Spelling Challenge 8
occurred

Spelling Challenge 9
village

Spelling Challenge 10
surprise

Spelling Challenge 11
generally

Spelling Challenge 12
cemetery

Spelling Challenge 13
existence

Spelling Challenge 14
accommodate

Spelling Challenge 15
humorous

Spelling Challenge 16
pronunciation

Spelling Challenge 17
occasion

Spelling Challenge 18
recommend

Spelling Challenge 19
disappoint

Spelling Challenge 20
beginning

Age of Words Challenge 1
1. kettle
2. tent
3. antenna

Age of Words Challenge 2
1. candle
2. voyage
3. phony

Age of Words Challenge 3
1. dish
2. narcotic
3. voyeur

Age of Words Challenge 4
1. play
2. suit
3. aquifer

Age of Words Challenge 5
1. dwarf
2. prune
3. barrette

Age of Words Challenge 6
1. stride
2. abstain
3. calibrator

Age of Words Challenge 7
1. greet
2. toothache
3. ethanol

Age of Words Challenge 8
1. key
2. chemistry
3. antilog

Age of Words Challenge 9
1. yellow
2. wrangle
3. nifty

Age of Words Challenge 10
1. iron
2. freeze
3. escalator

Age of Words Challenge 11
1. tough
2. warrior
3. malnourished

Age of Words Challenge 12
1. half
2. alley
3. antonym

Age of Words Challenge 13
1. tide
2. princess
3. nosedive

Age of Words Challenge 14
1. flea
2. pamper
3. mindset

Age of Words Challenge 15
1. thief
2. meridian
3. agnostic

Age of Words Challenge 16
1. wonder
2. windmill
3. tendinitis

Age of Words Challenge 17
1. gold
2. gag
3. malarkey

Age of Words Challenge 18
1. hook
2. vengeance
3. spoonerism

Age of Words Challenge 19
1. hat
2. adulation
3. internment

Age of Words Challenge 20
1. birch
2. verdict
3. amputee

Chapter 14:
Word Know-It-All

Pick the Best Definition for Allied
a. Related

Pick the Best Definition for Armistice
b. A truce

Pick the Best Definition for Disbar
a. To expel from the legal profession

Pick the Best Definition for Truant
a. A student who stays away from school without permission

Pick the Best Definition for Lye
b. A strong alkaline substance used in making soap

Pick the Best Definition for Nip
c. A small amount of liquor

Pick the Best Definition for Aperture
c. An opening

Pick the Best Definition for Mediate
c. To settle differences between conflicting parties

Pick the Best Definition for Assent

c. Consent

Pick the Best Definition for Disparage

b. To degrade

Pick the Best Definition for Barbiturate

a: A group of drugs that act as depressants

Pick the Best Definition for Altercation

a. A noisy, angry dispute

Pick the Best Definition for Amphetamine

b. Drug used as a stimulant

Pick the Best Definition for Aggregate

a. Total amount

Pick the Best Definition for Flit

c. To pass abruptly

Pick the Best Definition for Ampere

c. Unit of electric current

Pick the Best Definition for Mesosphere

a. Portion of the atmosphere from twenty to fifty miles above the earth

Pick the Best Definition for Au Gratin

a. With a cheese crust

Pick the Best Definition for Anterior

c. Located before in place or time

Pick the Best Definition for Alibi

c. An excuse

Pick the Best Definition for Bayou

b. A marshy inlet

Pick the Best Definition for Jaundice

c. Disorder with the symptom of yellowish skin

Pick the Best Definition for Alpha

a. First letter in the Greek alphabet

Pick the Best Definition for Transcribe

a. To make a written copy of

Pick the Best Definition for Avail

b. To be of use

Pick the Best Definition for Writhe

c. To twist and turn the body

Pick the Best Definition for Plague

c. Pestilence

Pick the Best Definition for Avow

c. Declare openly

Pick the Best Definition for Avoirdupois

a. System of weight measurement

Pick the Best Definition for Scaphoid

c. Shaped like a boat

Pick the Best Definition for Atomizer

a. Device for spraying liquid as a mist

Pick the Best Definition for Mesopause

c. Atmospheric area about fifty miles above the earth's surface

Pick the Best Definition for Alveolate

a. Pitted like a honeycomb

Pick the Best Definition for Quartan

a. Occurring every fourth day

Pick the Best Definition for Babushka

b. A type of scarf

Pick the Best Definition for Flout

b. To scorn or scoff

Pick the Best Definition for Quindecennial

b. A fifteenth anniversary

Pick the Best Definition for Cerement

c. A burial garment

Pick the Best Definition for Agora

a. A gathering place

Pick the Best Definition for Cespitose

c. Growing in clumps, like moss

Pick the Best Definition for Platitude

b. A trite remark

Pick the Best Definition for Quadruped

a. An animal with four feet

Pick the Best Definition for Distend

a. To become expanded

Pick the Best Definition for Zizith

b. The tassels worn on traditional garments by Jewish males

Pick the Best Definition for Anthracite

b. Hard coal

Pick the Best Definition for Quadrille

b. A dance of French origin

Pick the Best Definition for Gouache

b. A technique of painting using opaque watercolors

Pick the Best Definition for Placate

c. To appease

Pick the Best Definition for Baba

b. A rum cake usually made with raisins

Pick the Best Definition for Anabiosis

c. Moving again after apparent death

Pick the Best Definition for Ampoule

a. Container for a dose of medicine

Pick the Best Definition for Jackanapes

a. A mischievous child

Pick the Best Definition for Asperity

c. Harshness

Pick the Best Definition for Soliloquy

b. Talking to oneself

Pick the Best Definition for Abaft

c. Toward the stern

Pick the Best Definition for Rondo

b. A musical form in which a refrain recurs four times

Pick the Best Definition for Acephalous

a. Without a head

Pick the Best Definition for Jato

a. An aircraft takeoff assisted by an auxiliary jet

Pick the Best Definition for Nike

c. The Greek goddess of victory

Chapter 15: Phone Numbers

Placement
- first
- third
- fifth

Mammals
- moose
- horse
- tiger

Sport Areas
- track
- field
- court

Symphony
- viola
- cello
- flute

Bathroom
- towel
- basin
- brush

Fire
- spark
- flame
- ember

Close to the Ground
- snake
- worms
- gecko

Clothes
- shirt
- pants
- socks

Cuts
- sword
- knife
- blade

Sizes
- giant
- small
- large

Computer Peripherals
- mouse
- modem
- cable

Yard
- trees
- grass
- shrub

Measures
- meter
- liter
- ounce

On the Table
- spoon
- knife
- plate

Humor
- funny
- comic
- laugh

Landscape
- ridge
- hilly
- mound

Legal Tender
- moncy
- coins
- cents

See You in Court
- juror
- judge
- clerk

Dinner
- pasta
- salad
- drink

Body Joints
- elbow
- ankle
- wrist

Talk
- gossip
- rumors
- tattle

Colors
- yellow
- orange
- purple

Elements
- oxygen
- helium
- carbon

Taken
- ripoff
- stolen
- swiped

Composition
- poetry
- rhymes
- verses

Space
- galaxy
- planet
- Saturn

Teeth
- cavity
- braces
- dental

School
- grades
- pupils
- lesson

Films
- screen
- movies
- cinema

Vision
- retina
- cornea
- eyelid

Family
- sister
- father
- mother

Ha Ha Ha
- giggle
- guffaw
- cackle

Thief
- outlaw
- robber
- bandit

Speed
- rushed
- slowly
- faster

Time
- second
- minute
- decade

Sports
- soccer
- tennis
- hockey

Temperature
- cooler
- warmer
- hotter

In the Office
- copier
- pencil
- phones

Fruits
- banana
- grapes
- orange

Dogs
- beagle
- collie
- poodle

Chapter 16: Cryptograms

Cryptoquote Challenge 1
The problem is not that there are problems. The problem is expecting otherwise and thinking that having problems is a problem.

—*Theodore Rubin*

Cryptoquote Challenge 2
Every child is an artist. The problem is how to remain an artist once he grows up.

—*Pablo Picasso*

Cryptoquote Challenge 3
Progress always involves risk; you can't steal second base and keep your foot on first base.

—*Frederick Wilcox*

Cryptoquote Challenge 4
You're never as good as everyone tells you when you win, and you're never as bad as they say when you lose.

—*Lou Holtz*

Cryptoquote Challenge 5
Never doubt that a small group of thoughtful committed people can change the world: indeed it's the only thing that ever has!

—*Margaret Meade*

Cryptoquote Challenge 6
Kindness in words creates confidence. Kindness in thinking creates profoundness. Kindness in giving creates love.

—*Lao Tzu*

Cryptoquote Challenge 7
Always remember, others may hate you. But those who hate you don't win unless you hate them. And then you destroy yourself.

—*Richard M. Nixon*

Cryptoquote Challenge 8
I think that people want peace so much that one of these days governments had better get out of the way and let them have it.

—*Dwight D. Eisenhower*

Cryptoquote Challenge 9
The problems that exist in the world today cannot be solved by the level of thinking that created them.

—*Albert Einstein*

Cryptoquote Challenge 10
Remember happiness doesn't depend upon who you are or what you have; it depends solely on what you think.

—*Dale Carnegie*

Cryptoquote Challenge 11
They say a person needs just three things to be truly happy in this world: someone to love, something to do, and something to hope for.

—*Tom Bodett*

Cryptoquote Challenge 12
I am prepared to die, but there is no cause for which I am prepared to kill.

—*Mahatma Gandhi*

Cryptoquote Challenge 13
Wise men talk because they have something to say; fools, because they have to say something.

—*Plato*

Cryptoquote Challenge 14
The best way to cheer yourself is to try to cheer someone else up.

—*Mark Twain*

Cryptoquote Challenge 15
When you have confidence, you can have a lot of fun. And when you have fun, you can do amazing things.

—*Joe Namath*

Cryptoquote Challenge 16
If one is master of one thing and understands one thing well, one has at the same time, insight into and understanding of many things.

—*Vincent van Gogh*

Cryptoquote Challenge 17
I may not have gone where I intended to go, but I think I have ended up where I intended to be.

—*Douglas Adams*

Cryptoquote Challenge 18
You can discover more about a person in an hour of play than in a year of conversation.

—*Plato*

Cryptoquote Challenge 19
I have found the best way to give advice to your children is to find out what they want and then advise them to do it.

—*Harry S Truman*

Cryptoquote Challenge 20
The good people sleep much better at night than the bad people. Of course, the bad people enjoy the waking hours much more.

—*Woody Allen*

Cryptoquote Challenge 21
Today the real test of power is not capacity to make war but the capacity to prevent it.

—*Anne O'Hare McCormick*

Cryptoquote Challenge 22

Thinking is the enemy of creativity. It's self-conscious, and anything self-conscious is lousy. You can't try to do things. You simply must do things.

—*Ray Bradbury*

Cryptoquote Challenge 23

Our progress as a nation can be no swifter than our progress in education. The human mind is our fundamental resource.

—*John F. Kennedy*

Cryptoquote Challenge 24

The difference between the right word and the almost right word is the difference between lightning and a lightning bug.

—*Mark Twain*

Cryptoquote Challenge 25

A common mistake that people make when trying to design something completely foolproof is to underestimate the ingenuity of complete fools.

—*Douglas Adams*

Cryptoquote Challenge 26

We are shaped by our thoughts; we become what we think. When the mind is pure, joy follows like a shadow that never leaves.

—*Buddha*

Cryptoquote Challenge 27

The illiterate of the future will not be the person who cannot read. It will be the person who does not know how to learn.

—*Alvin Toffler*

Cryptoquote Challenge 28

Men can only be happy when they do not assume that the object of life is happiness.

—*George Orwell*

Cryptoquote Challenge 29

Success is not the key to happiness. Happiness is the key to success. If you love what you are doing, you will be successful.

—*Herman Cain*

Cryptoquote Challenge 30

Whatever you want to do, do it now. There are only so many tomorrows.

—*Michael Landon*

U.S. Holidays

Easter
Christmas
Thanksgiving
New Year's Day
Fourth of July
Memorial Day
Labor Day

Shakespeare

Taming of the Shrew
A Midsummer Night's Dream
Romeo and Juliet
Much Ado About Nothing
Hamlet
All's Well That Ends Well
Macbeth

Insects

hornet
ladybug
butterfly
locust
mosquito
cricket
grasshopper

Beatles Songs

"A Hard Day's Night"
"Love Me Do"
"Paperback Writer"
"Hey Jude"
"I Am the Walrus"
"Let It Be"
"I Want to Hold Your Hand"

Office Supplies

pencils
pens
paper
paperclips
scissors
ruler
stapler

Classic Literature

The Adventures of Tom Sawyer
Don Quixote
Dr. Jekyll and Mr. Hyde
The Scarlet Letter
A Tale of Two Cities
The Time Machine
Treasure Island

Gems

diamond
emerald
garnet
opal
ruby
sapphire
turquoise

Automobile

tires
windshield
steering wheel
glove compartment
radio
odometer
speedometer

U.S. National Parks

Grand Canyon
Yosemite
Yellowstone
Glacier Bay
Grand Teton

Rocky Mountain

Bryce Canyon

Movies

Finding Nemo

Bruce Almighty

Men in Black

Sweet Home Alabama

Planet of the Apes

A Beautiful Mind

American Beauty

Chapter 17: Word Numbers

Chronogram Challenge 1

- Knoxville (XVI)
- cider (CI)
- library (LI)

Chronogram Challenge 2

- excited (XCI)
- exit (XI)
- McIntosh (MCI)

Chronogram Challenge 3

- streamlined (MLI)
- summer (MM)
- anecdotes (CD)

Chronogram Challenge 4

- gumdrops (MD)
- mix (MIX)
- olives (LIV)

Chronogram Challenge 5

- handclaps (DCL)
- axles (XL)
- immigrants (MMI)

Chronogram Challenge 6

- mice (MI)
- excellent (XC)
- radii (DII)

Chronogram Challenge 7

- silvers (LV)
- foxlike (XLI)
- villages (VI)

Chronogram Challenge 8

- sandcastles (DC)
- elixirs (LIX)
- Hawaii (II)

Chronogram Challenge 9

- Nixon (IX)
- Hamlet (ML)
- Elvis (LVI)

Chronogram Challenge 10

- headlines (DLI)
- emcee (MC)
- skydive (DIV)

Number Name Chronogram: 2-10-8

The fancy FOOTWORK of the boxer is what made him a CONTENDER against the HEAVYWEIGHT champion.

Number Name Chronogram: 1-10-1

The epitaph "GONE but not FORGOTTEN" was etched in STONE.

Number Name Chronogram: 8-10-1

The ship carried FREIGHT that he INTENDED to sell in Canada for a lot of MONEY.

Number Name Chronogram: 2-10-2

Clint EASTWOOD played the policeman LIEUTENANT Speer in the movie *City Heat* which played on the ABC television NETWORK last night.

Number Name Chronogram: 1-1-1

The PRISONER felt very LONELY in solitary confinement after hearing that his trial was POSTPONED again.

Number Name Chronogram: 10-10-8

She held a PATENT for her invention of a radio ANTENNA that required a HEIGHT of only five feet.

Number Name Chronogram: 10-9-10

As we LISTENED to the lecture, the professor classified the dog as a CANINE and the KITTEN as a feline.

Number Name Chronogram: 8-1-10

The WEIGHT of the load made the porter's BONES ache and required his full ATTENTION to keep it balanced.

Number Name Chronogram: 10-1-1

She OFTEN told him to please PHONE me SOONER rather than later.

Number Name Chronogram: 1-8-10

NONE of his SLEIGHT of hand tricks worked when he was wearing MITTENS that covered his fingers.

Cryptarithm Challenge 1

There are twenty possible solutions:

8+692=700

8+592=600

8+492=500

8+392=400

7+593=600

7+493=500

7+193=200

6+794=800

6+294=300

6+194=200
4+796=800
4+296=300
4+196=200
3+597=600
3+497=500
3+197=200
2+698=700
2+598=600
2+498=500
2+398=400

Cryptarithm Challenge 2
There are six possible solutions:
868+747=1,615
848+565=1,413
838+474=1,312
767+848=1,615
545+868=1,413
434+878=1,312

Cryptarithm Challenge 3
There are sixteen possible solutions:
467+467=934
457+457=914
427+427=854
417+417=834
407+407=814
286+286=572
236+236=472
216+216=432
206+206=412
482+482=964
452+452=904
432+432=864
291+291=582
281+281=562
271+271=542
231+231=462

Cryptarithm Challenge 4
There are sixteen possible solutions:
8,366+7,554=15,920
7,366+8,554=15,920
8,766+5,443=14,209

5,766+8,443=14,209
8,355+7,669=16,024
7,355+8,669=16,024
6,844+5,229=12,073
5,844+6,229=12,073
7,944+5,336=13,280
5,944+7,336=13,280
9,233+5,447=14,680
5,233+9,447=14,680
7,833+4,226=12,059
4,833+7,226=12,059
8,433+7,662=16,095
7,433+8,662=16,095

Cryptarithm Challenge 5
There are seven possible solutions:
3,779+4,578=8,357
3,448+2,946=6,394
7,556+2,159=9,715
4,115+2,316=6,431
7,224+1,528=8,752
4,112+5,319=9,431
2,771+3,476=6,247

Cryptarithm Challenge 6
There are eighteen possible solutions:
6,849+6,855=13,704
8,649+8,655=17,304
8,349+8,355=16,704
6,349+6,355=12,704
7,639+7,644=15,283
8,529+8,533=17,062
5,429+5,433=10,862
6,458+6,477=12,935
6,528+6,544=13,072
5,328+5,344=10,672
9,237+9,266=18,503
8,425+8,477=16,902
9,274+9,233=18,507
8,274+8,233=16,507
6,702+6,788=13,490
7,302+7,388=14,690
5,382+5,366=10,748
9,362+9,344=18,706

Cryptarithm Challenge 7
There are two possible solutions:
94,085+64,773=158,858
64,085+94,773=158,858

Cryptarithm Challenge 8
There are fifteen possible solutions:
9,185+35,891=45,076
9,185+25,891=35,076
9,364+14,693=24,057
9,184+24,891=34,075
9,183+53,891=63,074
9,182+52,891=62,073
9,182+42,891=52,073
9,761+21,697=31,458
9,741+51,497=61,238
9,631+41,396=51,027
9,581+21,895=31,476
9,541+71,495=81,036
9,381+51,893=61,274
9,361+71,693=81,054
9,271+41,792=51,063

Cryptarithm Challenge 9
There are ten possible solutions:
4,359+8,208=12,567
5,609+8,428=14,037
4,789+6,036=10,825
7,829+6,406=14,235
7,809+4,254=12,063
4,258+9,309=13,567
9,268+5,405=14,673
6,274+9,509=15,783
8,053+6,476=14,529
3,562+7,087=10,649

Cryptarithm Challenge 10
There are fourteen possible solutions:
37,409+15,289=52,698
17,409+35,289=52,698
47,209+16,389=63,598
17,209+46,389=63,598
70,536+18,926=89,462
10,536+78,926=89,462
73,645+19,205=92,850

13,645+79,205=92,850
51,682+39,042=90,724
31,682+59,042=90,724
40,691+37,821=78,512
30,691+47,821=78,512
47,091+38,521=85,612
37,091+48,521=85,612

Chapter 18: Word Logic

Dr. Rational Challenge 1
Dr. Rational likes seven, because if the first letter of *seven* is removed another word is formed.

Dr. Rational Challenge 2
Dr. Rational likes Bridget, because *Bridget* ends with the letter *t*.

Dr. Rational Challenge 3
Dr. Rational likes evil, because *evil* spells a word when reversed (live).

Dr. Rational Challenge 4
Dr. Rational likes saws, because *saws* contains the letter *w*.

Dr. Rational Challenge 5
Dr. Rational likes noon, because *noon* begins with two letters that are consecutive in the alphabet.

Dr. Rational Challenge 6
Dr. Rational likes anagrams, because *anagrams* has three *a's*.

Dr. Rational Challenge 7
Dr. Rational likes cherries, because *cherries* contains the word *her*.

Dr. Rational Challenge 8
Dr. Rational likes Ohio, because *Ohio* begins and ends with the same letter.

Dr. Rational Challenge 9
Dr. Rational likes tales, because *tales* is an anagram of the word *stale*.

Dr. Rational Challenge 10
Dr. Rational likes hymns, because *hymns* contains *y* used as a vowel.

Dr. Rational Challenge 11
Dr. Rational likes cookbooks, because *cookbooks* has a letter used four times.

Dr. Rational Challenge 12
Dr. Rational likes audiotape, because *audiotape* has all of these letters: *a, e, i, o,* and *u*.

Dr. Rational Challenge 13
Dr. Rational likes Ann, because *Ann* uses only two letters.

Dr. Rational Challenge 14
Dr. Rational likes augite, because *augite* starts with an abbreviation for a month.

Dr. Rational Challenge 15
Dr. Rational likes cute, because if the last letter of *cute* is removed another word is formed.

Letter States Challenge 1
Ohio
Letter States Challenge 2
Oregon
Letter States Challenge 3
Kansas
Letter States Challenge 4
Illinois
Letter States Challenge 5
Vermont
Letter States Challenge 6
Idaho
Letter States Challenge 7
Nevada
Letter States Challenge 8
Montana
Letter States Challenge 9
Alaska
Letter States Challenge 10
Arizona
Letter States Challenge 11
Colorado
Letter States Challenge 12
Texas

Chapter 19: The Riddler

Riddle of the Sphinx
A man who crawls as a child, walks upright in his prime, and uses a cane in old age.

Ends in -GRY
Language, because it is the third word in the phrase "the English language."

Children
The stars

Sings
A bell

Lawyer, Soldier, Sailor
Yvan, a reversal of the word navy

Fishermen
The fisherman had been infected with lice. The lice that they caught were picked off and left behind, and the lice that they did not catch were unwittingly carried away.

Begin and End
The letter *e*.

Long and Short
Time

Flying
Smoke

Touch Me
Heart

Three Letters
Few

Waves Over Me
Oyster

Related
"That man" is my son.

Behead
Stable

Devoured
Candle

The Rich Require
Nothing

Two and Two
A kiss

A Breed Unfit
Mule

Breathe
Bellows

Sixty
A woman in labor with twins

Never and Always
Tomorrow

Strange Indeed
A drum

Airy Creatures
Vowels

Eat
Time

Clamorous
A vacuum cleaner

A Yellow Fork
Lightning

Play
Musicians

Suspended in Air
The letter *i*

Under the Sea
An anchor

Up and Down
everything is under control
man overboard
long underwear

Neighbors
life after death
he's beside himself
I'm bigger than you

Within
the inside scoop
a big fish in a small pond
a stitch in time

Backwords
glance backwards
he ran backwards and forwards
looking backwards over the years

Double
paradise
all in all
despair

Broken
a house divided
scrambled eggs
coffee break

Sports
tennis shoes (ten issues)
out in leftfield
double dribble

Letters Only
water (H to O)
anemone (an M and E)
noel (No L)

Phraseology
I'm overworked and underpaid.
Too wise you are, too wise you be, I
  see you are too wise for me.

It's a small world after all.

Stuck Key
The Andes
excuse
Tennessee

Chapter 20: Advanced Challenges

Hemingway Books
1. *The Old Man and the Sea*
2. *The Sun Also Rises*
3. *A Farewell to Arms*

Rodgers and Hammerstein
1. *State Fair*
2. *The Sound of Music*
3. *South Pacific*

1980s Television Shows
1. *The Dukes of Hazzard*
2. *The Love Boat*
3. *Little House on the Prairie*

Elvis Presley Songs
1. "Return To Sender"
2. "Love Me Tender"
3. "Are You Lonesome Tonight?"

Harrison Ford Movies
1. *Raiders of the Lost Ark*
2. *Clear and Present Danger*
3. *Air Force One*

Multiple Transaddition Challenge 1
1. cats
2. tacos
3. actors
4. coaster
5. ancestor

Multiple Transaddition Challenge 2
1. rose

2. horse
3. chores
4. roaches
5. poachers

Multiple Transaddition Challenge 3

1. care
2. trace
3. nectar
4. certain
5. clarinet

Multiple Transaddition Challenge 4

1. life
2. rifle
3. filter
4. trifles
5. filberts

Multiple Transaddition Challenge 5

1. cent
2. scent
3. insect
4. clients
5. stencils

TICKET to TRAINS

TICKET, PICKET, PICKED, PECKED, PEAKED, BEAKED, BRAKED, BRACED, TRACED, TRACES, TRACTS, TRAITS, TRAINS

FASTER to SLOWER

FASTER, FESTER, FEATER, FEARER, FEARED, FLARED, FLAWED, FLOWED, FLOWER, SLOWER

CROOKS to CRIMES

CROOKS, CROCKS, CRICKS, PRICKS, PRICES, PRIMES, CRIMES

GOLFER to SPORTS

GOLFER, WOLFER, WOOFER, HOOFER, HOOKER, COOKER, CHOKER, CHOKES, CHORES, SHORES, SPORES, SPORTS

LISTEN to BUGLER

LISTEN, LISTER, LITTER, BITTER, BUTTER, BUTLER, BUGLER

Sequence: ESSO

accessories, accessorize, accessory, aggressor, assessor, compressor, confessor, coprocessor, depressor, dispossessor, espresso, intercessor, intercessory, lesson, lessor, microprocessor, multiprocessor, oppressor, possessor, predecessor, processor, professor, professorial, professorially, professorship, repressor, stressor, successor, suppressor, transgressor

Sequence: RASE

catchphrase, erase, erased, eraser, esterase, extrasensory, paraphrase, paraphrased, paraphraser, phrase, phrased, phraseless, phrasemaker, phraseologist, phraseology, polymerase, rephrase

Sequence: EASU

admeasure, countermeasure, countermeasures, displeasure, immeasurable, immeasurableness, immeasurably, measurability, measurable, measurably, measure, measured, measureless, measurement, measurer, measures, measuring, pleasurable, pleasurably, pleasure, treasure, treasured, treasurer, treasuries, treasuring, treasury, unmeasurable, unmeasured

Sequence: ENCI

agencies, commencing, conferencing, constituencies, contingencies, currencies, dependencies, emergencies, encipher, encircle, encircled, encirclement, encircling, experiencing, fencing, frequencies, influencing, pencil, penciled, penciling, presidencies, sentencing, sequencing, silencing, stencil, stenciled, stenciler, stenciling, teleconferencing, tendencies, videoconferencing

Sequence: NDAR

boundaries, boundary, calendar, gendarme, gendarmerie, legendary, mandarin, nonstandard, quandaries, quandary, secondaries, secondarily, secondary, standard, standardization, standardize, standardized, standards, substandard

Sequence: EALI

appealing, appealingly, concealing, congealing, corporeality, dealing, dealings, ethereality, healing, idealism, idealist, idealistic, ideality, idealization, idealize, idealized, idealizing, pealing, realign, realism, realist, realistic, realistically, reality, realizable, realization, realize, realized, realizer, realizing, repealing, revealing, sealing, squealing, stealing, surrealism, surrealist, surrealistic, unappealing, unappealingly, unrealistic, unrealistically, unreality, unrealizable, unrealized

Quintuplets Challenge 1

FIRE: fireworks, wildfire, fireman, campfire, crossfire

Quintuplets Challenge 2

HOT: hotbed, hot plate, hotcake, red-hot, hotwire

THE EVERYTHING WORD GAMES CHALLENGE BOOK

Quintuplets Challenge 3

STAR: starfish, starlight, superstar, starship, stargaze

Quintuplets Challenge 4

FALL: nightfall, fallback, pitfall, fallout, waterfall

Quintuplets Challenge 5

MEAL: piecemeal, mealtime, cornmeal, mealworm, oatmeal

Spaceless Cryptoquote Challenge 1

It's a recession when your neighbor loses his job; it's a depression when you lose yours.

—*Harry S Truman*

Spaceless Cryptoquote Challenge 2

The happiest moments of my life have been the few which I have passed at home in the bosom of my family.

—*Thomas Jefferson*

Spaceless Cryptoquote Challenge 3

Because only if you've been in the deepest valley can you ever know how magnificent it is to be on the highest mountain.

—*Richard M. Nixon*

Spaceless Cryptoquote Challenge 4

Politics is supposed to be the second oldest profession. I have come to realize that it bears a very close resemblance to the first.

—*Ronald Reagan*

Spaceless Cryptoquote Challenge 5

My first wish is to see this plague of mankind, war, banished from the earth.

—*George Washington*

Appendix B

Web Sites for Puzzlers

Funster

A popular Web site for wordplay created by the author of this book. Includes multiplayer versions of some of the games presented here, including What's in a Name? and Word Know-It-All. Compete and chat with players from around the world.
www.funster.com

All-Star Puzzles

A nice collection of word games, including Anagrams and Cryptograms.
www.allstarpuzzles.com

Braingle

A Web site devoted to providing entertainment for people who like mental challenges. It has a range of games, including many word puzzles.
www.braingle.com

Discovery School's Puzzlemaker

Online software to create your own word puzzles. Brought to you by the Discovery Channel.
http://puzzlemaker.school.discovery.com

Fun-with-words.com

A large collection of word games including Hangman, Anagrams, Rebuses, and many other forms of wordplay.
www.fun-with-words.com

OneLook Dictionary Search

Searches a growing list of online dictionaries and presents the results on one page. Allows you to search for a wildcard pattern (for example, all of the words ending with act.)
www.onelook.com

RhymeZone

Online tool to find words that rhyme. Can be used to create Inky Pinky puzzles like the ones in this book.
www.rhymezone.com

RiddleNut

A huge collection of riddles.
www.riddlenut.com

Thinks.com

A collection of fun games and pastimes, including a large wordplay section.
http://thinks.com

PhoneSpell

A simple Web site that will tell you what your phone number spells. Similar to the Phone Numbers puzzles in this book.
www.phonespell.com

Wordsmith.org

Includes the Internet Anagram Server that will anagram any given text. For example, it will rearrange the letters in your name to spell words.
http://wordsmith.org

Yahoo! Games

One of the most popular places for online games. Includes a collection of word games.
http://games.yahoo.com

The EVERYTHING Series!

BUSINESS & PERSONAL FINANCE

Everything® Accounting Book
Everything® Budgeting Book
Everything® Business Planning Book
Everything® Coaching and Mentoring Book
Everything® Fundraising Book
Everything® Get Out of Debt Book
Everything® Grant Writing Book
Everything® Guide to Personal Finance for Single Mothers
Everything® Home-Based Business Book, 2nd Ed.
Everything® Homebuying Book, 2nd Ed.
Everything® Homeselling Book, 2nd Ed.
Everything® Improve Your Credit Book
Everything® Investing Book, 2nd Ed.
Everything® Landlording Book
Everything® Leadership Book
Everything® Managing People Book, 2nd Ed.
Everything® Negotiating Book
Everything® Online Auctions Book
Everything® Online Business Book
Everything® Personal Finance Book
Everything® Personal Finance in Your 20s and 30s Book
Everything® Project Management Book
Everything® Real Estate Investing Book
Everything® Retirement Planning Book
Everything® Robert's Rules Book, $7.95
Everything® Selling Book
Everything® Start Your Own Business Book, 2nd Ed.
Everything® Wills & Estate Planning Book

COOKING

Everything® Barbecue Cookbook
Everything® Bartender's Book, $9.95
Everything® Cheese Book
Everything® Chinese Cookbook
Everything® Classic Recipes Book
Everything® Cocktail Parties and Drinks Book
Everything® College Cookbook
Everything® Cooking for Baby and Toddler Book
Everything® Cooking for Two Cookbook
Everything® Diabetes Cookbook
Everything® Easy Gourmet Cookbook
Everything® Fondue Cookbook
Everything® Fondue Party Book
Everything® Gluten-Free Cookbook
Everything® Glycemic Index Cookbook
Everything® Grilling Cookbook

Everything® Healthy Meals in Minutes Cookbook
Everything® Holiday Cookbook
Everything® Indian Cookbook
Everything® Italian Cookbook
Everything® Low-Carb Cookbook
Everything® Low-Fat High-Flavor Cookbook
Everything® Low-Salt Cookbook
Everything® Meals for a Month Cookbook
Everything® Mediterranean Cookbook
Everything® Mexican Cookbook
Everything® No Trans Fat Cookbook
Everything® One-Pot Cookbook
Everything® Pizza Cookbook
Everything® Quick and Easy 30-Minute, 5-Ingredient Cookbook
Everything® Quick Meals Cookbook
Everything® Slow Cooker Cookbook
Everything® Slow Cooking for a Crowd Cookbook
Everything® Soup Cookbook
Everything® Stir-Fry Cookbook
Everything® Tex-Mex Cookbook
Everything® Thai Cookbook
Everything® Vegetarian Cookbook
Everything® Wild Game Cookbook
Everything® Wine Book, 2nd Ed.

GAMES

Everything® 15-Minute Sudoku Book, $9.95
Everything® 30-Minute Sudoku Book, $9.95
Everything® Blackjack Strategy Book
Everything® Brain Strain Book, $9.95
Everything® Bridge Book
Everything® Card Games Book
Everything® Card Tricks Book, $9.95
Everything® Casino Gambling Book, 2nd Ed.
Everything® Chess Basics Book
Everything® Craps Strategy Book
Everything® Crossword and Puzzle Book
Everything® Crossword Challenge Book
Everything® Crosswords for the Beach Book, $9.95
Everything® Cryptograms Book, $9.95
Everything® Easy Crosswords Book
Everything® Easy Kakuro Book, $9.95
Everything® Easy Large Print Crosswords Book
Everything® Games Book, 2nd Ed.
Everything® Giant Sudoku Book, $9.95
Everything® Kakuro Challenge Book, $9.95
Everything® Large-Print Crossword Challenge Book

Everything® Large-Print Crosswords Book
Everything® Lateral Thinking Puzzles Book, $9.95
Everything® Mazes Book
Everything® Movie Crosswords Book, $9.95
Everything® Online Poker Book, $12.95
Everything® Pencil Puzzles Book, $9.95
Everything® Poker Strategy Book
Everything® Pool & Billiards Book
Everything® Sports Crosswords Book, $9.95
Everything® Test Your IQ Book, $9.95
Everything® Texas Hold 'Em Book, $9.95
Everything® Travel Crosswords Book, $9.95
Everything® Word Games Challenge Book
Everything® Word Scramble Book
Everything® Word Search Book

HEALTH

Everything® Alzheimer's Book
Everything® Diabetes Book
Everything® Health Guide to Adult Bipolar Disorder
Everything® Health Guide to Controlling Anxiety
Everything® Health Guide to Fibromyalgia
Everything® Health Guide to Postpartum Care
Everything® Health Guide to Thyroid Disease
Everything® Hypnosis Book
Everything® Low Cholesterol Book
Everything® Massage Book
Everything® Menopause Book
Everything® Nutrition Book
Everything® Reflexology Book
Everything® Stress Management Book

HISTORY

Everything® American Government Book
Everything® American History Book, 2nd Ed.
Everything® Civil War Book
Everything® Freemasons Book
Everything® Irish History & Heritage Book
Everything® Middle East Book

HOBBIES

Everything® Candlemaking Book
Everything® Cartooning Book
Everything® Coin Collecting Book
Everything® Drawing Book
Everything® Family Tree Book, 2nd Ed.
Everything® Knitting Book
Everything® Knots Book
Everything® Photography Book

Everything® Quilting Book
Everything® Scrapbooking Book
Everything® Sewing Book
Everything® Soapmaking Book, 2nd Ed.
Everything® Woodworking Book

HOME IMPROVEMENT

Everything® Feng Shui Book
Everything® Feng Shui Decluttering Book, $9.95
Everything® Fix-It Book
Everything® Home Decorating Book
Everything® Home Storage Solutions Book
Everything® Homebuilding Book
Everything® Organize Your Home Book

KIDS' BOOKS

All titles are $7.95

Everything® Kids' Animal Puzzle & Activity Book
Everything® Kids' Baseball Book, 4th Ed.
Everything® Kids' Bible Trivia Book
Everything® Kids' Bugs Book
Everything® Kids' Cars and Trucks Puzzle & Activity Book
Everything® Kids' Christmas Puzzle & Activity Book
Everything® Kids' Cookbook
Everything® Kids' Crazy Puzzles Book
Everything® Kids' Dinosaurs Book
Everything® Kids' First Spanish Puzzle and Activity Book
Everything® Kids' Gross Cookbook
Everything® Kids' Gross Hidden Pictures Book
Everything® Kids' Gross Jokes Book
Everything® Kids' Gross Mazes Book
Everything® Kids' Gross Puzzle and Activity Book
Everything® Kids' Halloween Puzzle & Activity Book
Everything® Kids' Hidden Pictures Book
Everything® Kids' Horses Book
Everything® Kids' Joke Book
Everything® Kids' Knock Knock Book
Everything® Kids' Learning Spanish Book
Everything® Kids' Math Puzzles Book
Everything® Kids' Mazes Book
Everything® Kids' Money Book
Everything® Kids' Nature Book
Everything® Kids' Pirates Puzzle and Activity Book
Everything® Kids' Presidents Book
Everything® Kids' Princess Puzzle and Activity Book
Everything® Kids' Puzzle Book
Everything® Kids' Riddles & Brain Teasers Book
Everything® Kids' Science Experiments Book
Everything® Kids' Sharks Book
Everything® Kids' Soccer Book
Everything® Kids' States Book
Everything® Kids' Travel Activity Book

KIDS' STORY BOOKS

Everything® Fairy Tales Book

LANGUAGE

Everything® Conversational Japanese Book with CD, $19.95
Everything® French Grammar Book
Everything® French Phrase Book, $9.95
Everything® French Verb Book, $9.95
Everything® German Practice Book with CD, $19.95
Everything® Inglés Book
Everything® Intermediate Spanish Book with CD, $19.95
Everything® Learning Brazilian Portuguese Book with CD, $19.95
Everything® Learning French Book
Everything® Learning German Book
Everything® Learning Italian Book
Everything® Learning Latin Book
Everything® Learning Spanish Book with CD, 2nd Edition, $19.95
Everything® Russian Practice Book with CD, $19.95
Everything® Sign Language Book
Everything® Spanish Grammar Book
Everything® Spanish Phrase Book, $9.95
Everything® Spanish Practice Book with CD, $19.95
Everything® Spanish Verb Book, $9.95
Everything® Speaking Mandarin Chinese Book with CD, $19.95

MUSIC

Everything® Drums Book with CD, $19.95
Everything® Guitar Book with CD, 2nd Edition, $19.95
Everything® Guitar Chords Book with CD, $19.95
Everything® Home Recording Book
Everything® Music Theory Book with CD, $19.95
Everything® Reading Music Book with CD, $19.95
Everything® Rock & Blues Guitar Book with CD, $19.95
Everything® Rock and Blues Piano Book with CD, $19.95
Everything® Songwriting Book

NEW AGE

Everything® Astrology Book, 2nd Ed.
Everything® Birthday Personology Book
Everything® Dreams Book, 2nd Ed.
Everything® Love Signs Book, $9.95
Everything® Numerology Book
Everything® Paganism Book
Everything® Palmistry Book
Everything® Psychic Book
Everything® Reiki Book

Everything® Sex Signs Book, $9.95
Everything® Tarot Book, 2nd Ed.
Everything® Toltec Wisdom Book
Everything® Wicca and Witchcraft Book

PARENTING

Everything® Baby Names Book, 2nd Ed.
Everything® Baby Shower Book
Everything® Baby's First Year Book
Everything® Birthing Book
Everything® Breastfeeding Book
Everything® Father-to-Be Book
Everything® Father's First Year Book
Everything® Get Ready for Baby Book
Everything® Get Your Baby to Sleep Book, $9.95
Everything® Getting Pregnant Book
Everything® Guide to Raising a One-Year-Old
Everything® Guide to Raising a Two-Year-Old
Everything® Homeschooling Book
Everything® Mother's First Year Book
Everything® Parent's Guide to Childhood Illnesses
Everything® Parent's Guide to Children and Divorce
Everything® Parent's Guide to Children with ADD/ADHD
Everything® Parent's Guide to Children with Asperger's Syndrome
Everything® Parent's Guide to Children with Autism
Everything® Parent's Guide to Children with Bipolar Disorder
Everything® Parent's Guide to Children with Depression
Everything® Parent's Guide to Children with Dyslexia
Everything® Parent's Guide to Children with Juvenile Diabetes
Everything® Parent's Guide to Positive Discipline
Everything® Parent's Guide to Raising a Successful Child
Everything® Parent's Guide to Raising Boys
Everything® Parent's Guide to Raising Girls
Everything® Parent's Guide to Raising Siblings
Everything® Parent's Guide to Sensory Integration Disorder
Everything® Parent's Guide to Tantrums
Everything® Parent's Guide to the Strong-Willed Child
Everything® Parenting a Teenager Book
Everything® Potty Training Book, $9.95
Everything® Pregnancy Book, 3rd Ed.
Everything® Pregnancy Fitness Book
Everything® Pregnancy Nutrition Book
Everything® Pregnancy Organizer, 2nd Ed., $16.95
Everything® Toddler Activities Book
Everything® Toddler Book

Everything® Tween Book
Everything® Twins, Triplets, and More Book

PETS

Everything® Aquarium Book
Everything® Boxer Book
Everything® Cat Book, 2nd Ed.
Everything® Chihuahua Book
Everything® Dachshund Book
Everything® Dog Book
Everything® Dog Health Book
Everything® Dog Obedience Book
Everything® Dog Owner's Organizer, $16.95
Everything® Dog Training and Tricks Book
Everything® German Shepherd Book
Everything® Golden Retriever Book
Everything® Horse Book
Everything® Horse Care Book
Everything® Horseback Riding Book
Everything® Labrador Retriever Book
Everything® Poodle Book
Everything® Pug Book
Everything® Puppy Book
Everything® Rottweiler Book
Everything® Small Dogs Book
Everything® Tropical Fish Book
Everything® Yorkshire Terrier Book

REFERENCE

Everything® American Presidents Book
Everything® Blogging Book
Everything® Build Your Vocabulary Book
Everything® Car Care Book
Everything® Classical Mythology Book
Everything® Da Vinci Book
Everything® Divorce Book
Everything® Einstein Book
Everything® Enneagram Book
Everything® Etiquette Book, 2nd Ed.
Everything® Inventions and Patents Book
Everything® Mafia Book
Everything® Philosophy Book
Everything® Pirates Book
Everything® Psychology Book

RELIGION

Everything® Angels Book
Everything® Bible Book
Everything® Buddhism Book
Everything® Catholicism Book
Everything® Christianity Book
Everything® Gnostic Gospels Book
Everything® History of the Bible Book
Everything® Jesus Book

Everything® Jewish History & Heritage Book
Everything® Judaism Book
Everything® Kabbalah Book
Everything® Koran Book
Everything® Mary Book
Everything® Mary Magdalene Book
Everything® Prayer Book
Everything® Saints Book, 2nd Ed.
Everything® Torah Book
Everything® Understanding Islam Book
Everything® World's Religions Book
Everything® Zen Book

SCHOOL & CAREERS

Everything® Alternative Careers Book
Everything® Career Tests Book
Everything® College Major Test Book
Everything® College Survival Book, 2nd Ed.
Everything® Cover Letter Book, 2nd Ed.
Everything® Filmmaking Book
Everything® Get-a-Job Book, 2nd Ed.
Everything® Guide to Being a Paralegal
Everything® Guide to Being a Personal Trainer
Everything® Guide to Being a Real Estate Agent
Everything® Guide to Being a Sales Rep
Everything® Guide to Careers in Health Care
Everything® Guide to Careers in Law Enforcement
Everything® Guide to Government Jobs
Everything® Guide to Starting and Running a Restaurant
Everything® Job Interview Book
Everything® New Nurse Book
Everything® New Teacher Book
Everything® Paying for College Book
Everything® Practice Interview Book
Everything® Resume Book, 2nd Ed.
Everything® Study Book

SELF-HELP

Everything® Dating Book, 2nd Ed.
Everything® Great Sex Book
Everything® Self-Esteem Book
Everything® Tantric Sex Book

SPORTS & FITNESS

Everything® Easy Fitness Book
Everything® Running Book
Everything® Weight Training Book

TRAVEL

Everything® Family Guide to Cruise Vacations
Everything® Family Guide to Hawaii
Everything® Family Guide to Las Vegas, 2nd Ed.
Everything® Family Guide to Mexico
Everything® Family Guide to New York City, 2nd Ed.
Everything® Family Guide to RV Travel & Campgrounds
Everything® Family Guide to the Caribbean
Everything® Family Guide to the Walt Disney World Resort®, Universal Studios®, and Greater Orlando, 4th Ed.
Everything® Family Guide to Timeshares
Everything® Family Guide to Washington D.C., 2nd Ed.

WEDDINGS

Everything® Bachelorette Party Book, $9.95
Everything® Bridesmaid Book, $9.95
Everything® Destination Wedding Book
Everything® Elopement Book, $9.95
Everything® Father of the Bride Book, $9.95
Everything® Groom Book, $9.95
Everything® Mother of the Bride Book, $9.95
Everything® Outdoor Wedding Book
Everything® Wedding Book, 3rd Ed.
Everything® Wedding Checklist, $9.95
Everything® Wedding Etiquette Book, $9.95
Everything® Wedding Organizer, 2nd Ed., $16.95
Everything® Wedding Shower Book, $9.95
Everything® Wedding Vows Book, $9.95
Everything® Wedding Workout Book
Everything® Weddings on a Budget Book, $9.95

WRITING

Everything® Creative Writing Book
Everything® Get Published Book, 2nd Ed.
Everything® Grammar and Style Book
Everything® Guide to Magazine Writing
Everything® Guide to Writing a Book Proposal
Everything® Guide to Writing a Novel
Everything® Guide to Writing Children's Books
Everything® Guide to Writing Copy
Everything® Guide to Writing Research Papers
Everything® Screenwriting Book
Everything® Writing Poetry Book
Everything® Writing Well Book